SEX BEGINS IN THE KITCHEN

Renewing Emotional and Physical Intimacy in Marriage

Dr. Kevin Leman

Regal Books

A Division of G/L Publications
Ventura, CA U.S.A.

The foreign language publishing of all Regal books is under the direction of GLINT. GLINT provides financial and technical help for the adaptation, translation and publishing of books in more than 85 languages for millions of people worldwide. For information regarding translation, contact: GLINT, P.O. Box 6688, Ventura, California 93006.

Second Printing, 1981

Published by Regal Books
A Division of GL Publications
Ventura, California 93006
Printed in U.S.A.

Library of Congress Catalog Card No. 80-54004
ISBN 0-8307-0787-5
Code Number 5109203

Contents

Dedication

To my wife Bucky—
My richest blessing

Acknowledgements

Thank You

To Sue Kent for her invaluable assistance in the preparation of my manuscript;

To Carol Lacy, my editor, for her perceptive contributions and her willingness to share her skills so beautifully;

To Dr. Oscar Christensen for influencing my professional life so greatly;

To my parents, John and May Leman, my brother Jack Leman, and my sister Sally Chall for their encouragement and love;

To the treasures of my life, daughters Holly, Kristin, and son Kevin for bringing me such great joy, comfort and love;

And thank *you* for buying this book. Without people like you there wouldn't be any successful books or authors.

ONE

To the Kitchen

It's one of those Friday nights when each member of the family has something to do. The two teenagers and their nine-year-old brother are going to the high school football game. It's Dad's night to bowl and Mom has to go to church to work on decorations for a mother-daughter banquet coming up the following evening. At 6:30 everybody flies out of the house toward their separate destinations.

Some three hours later, Mom is driving home from the church and all of a sudden it hits her! The dishes! When she left, the kitchen was an absolute mess, the dishes were left on the kitchen table . . . Everyone was in too much of a hurry.

As she drives along she weighs the advisability of doing the dishes as soon as she gets home; or should she wait until morning? She decides it would be too much to face the dishes in the morning so she'll conquer them when she gets home. She pulls into the driveway, gets out of the car, walks up on the porch, unlocks the front door and marches through the family room into the kitchen. She stops dead in her tracks as she sees a beautiful, sparkling-clean kitchen. She turns around, walks out of the house, checks the number over the front door. This is the right address. She walks back into the house just in time to see her husband hanging up the wet dish towels in the laundry room. SEX BEGINS IN THE KITCHEN.

Catchy title, isn't it? Sort of makes me frisky just to think about it. That's what this book is about—sex *does* begin in the kitchen; not at the point of the old proverb, "The way to a man's heart is through his stomach," but when *he* washes a sink full of dirty dishes just because they need doing and *she* already has more work than she can handle; or when *she* carries out the garbage because *he's* happily engrossed in the best football game of the season; or when *she* pools her income with his for the household budget—financial partnership, not "my own money and his money," (or more often than not, "my money and *our* money"). Or when caring for the kids is both their responsibility, not "her job."

Sex Begins in the Kitchen is premised on the ideal that your mate ought to be the Number One priority in life; that a good marital relationship is based upon pleasing each other, being sensitive and tuned-in to each other's emotional—as well as sexual—needs. This book concerns itself with our need to be intimate with each other as husband and wife, to share our most intimate thoughts and feelings; to come together as *one* in marriage, both emotionally and physically.

Unfortunately, in most marriages, couples live a "married-singles" life-style. In many marriages, after the bedroom door closes, nothing happens. And if sex does take place, it only occurs as a ritual or duty, typically in the bedroom, squeezed in after the late news and before "Johnny Carson."

It is not the result of a whole day full of affection, consideration, love and one-ness.

Now this isn't to say that on that Friday night when Dad
did the dishes before Mom got home that he was going to be
rewarded with sex with Mom. However, Mom's feelings had
to be, "Hey! What a neat experience to walk in and find that
Dad beat me home by a half-hour and was thoughtful
enough to clean the kitchen, just because it needed cleaning!" Most wives would interpret such an act as being per-
formed out of respect and love.

This kind of consideration toward each other can do
nothing but bring you closer together as man and wife.

In this particular situation sex did follow—an intimate
time of sharing and thanksgiving for each other. And it was
an indirect result of Dad recognizing a job that had to be done
and taking the time and making the commitment to do it.

What will it take to get your marriage to the place where
the primary motivation for all interaction between you and
your mate is love? What can you do to correct some of the
problems you now have?

In the following chapters I will share some of the things I
have discovered during my years of experience as a marriage
and family counselor and psychologist; more importantly,
during many years as a husband and father. I have watched
hundreds of couples come to grips with the fact that they
have to open up and take a good look at themselves in order
to have a satisfying marriage. Most of us don't really understand ourselves. But if we are going to share with our mate
and become one in marriage, we must be able to recognize
our own feelings, why we do what we do; we must understand what preconditioning we have received, what our

parents, teachers, churches and peers have programmed into us from an early age. We have to understand how these influences have affected our way of thinking and be able to select the things that will help us toward a one-ness in marriage. Also we need to know what it means to be committed to make needed changes.

In the chapter, "The Plight of Marriage" I will discuss why most marriages are in trouble so that you can recognize some danger signals. In the chapter entitled, "Who Did You Marry?" you will see how big a part your birth order plays in your marriage. In "Making the Pieces Fit" you will discover that you can never change another person, he must effect changes within himself, based solely on his own desire to change. But by changing your behavior you *allow* your mate to change. The only other choice is to learn to adjust to each other as you are.

One of the most important single factors in a marriage is communication. As a psychologist I find that men and women are basically afraid to tell each other who they are, to express their innermost thoughts, needs and feelings. I will cover this in chapter 5, "One Plus One Equals One."

"Nothing More Than Feelings" deals with our emotions, the feelings we all have, and how to recognize them and share them openly with our mates. In "How to Be Good and Angry" I will tell you how to deal with anger and frustration—another means of communication—in yourself and in your mate.

In the chapter, "Games Couples Play" you may find some portraits of yourself and your marriage. Most of us approach marriage as another game—competitive and sometimes violent. Looking at ourselves is not a painless job. Sometimes what we see can be pretty ugly. One section in the games chapter is entitled, "Children Are the Enemy." You will discover how we let those cute little "spittin' images" of ourselves come between us as husbands and wives. They can drive us up the wall!

Finally, "Ying-Yangs, Weenies, Talleywackers and 'The Thing' " is a real eye-opener chapter on sexual relationships. I have discovered that most men don't take the time to understand their wives at all, which leads to an unfulfilling sexual relationship for both of them.

We are being bombarded by experts trying to tell us that men and women are the same, that we are really moving toward a unisex society. The writings in this book will reflect that men and women are different; their needs are different. Happiness comes in recognizing and accepting these differences. The key to growth and enrichment in marriage is in reaching out and being able to touch each other in a very special way which conveys, "I understand how you feel and I'm going to do my very best to meet your needs."

I can't believe that 40-50 percent of all couples who walk up the flower-strewn aisle together and say their vows, do so expecting that their marriages will end up in divorce. Yet those are the disturbing statistics. Most of us *don't* approach marriage with an attitude of, "Well, if it doesn't work out we can always get a divorce." We all want a happy, successful, almost fairy-tale marriage and "happily ever-after" life. Yet it is ironic that with all the training and education available in today's society, our training for two of the most important tasks in life, marriage and parenthood, is almost non-existent.

Now you probably obtained this book because you want a more satisfying marriage or you know your marriage is already in trouble, or you are planning to marry soon and you don't want to be counted with the negative side of the statistics. I don't profess to have all the answers, but I guarantee that *Sex Begins in the Kitchen* will be practical and will give you some guidelines and insight into turning your relationship around, making your marriage what it should be.

Use this book to your advantage. If you find something in the book that you really like, underline it, put an asterisk next to it, dog-ear the page. If you find something that you don't believe in or you don't like, cross it out. If you find material that you can't relate to, rip the page out; but use the book to your advantage.

In many of the chapters I include exercises for you to do that will reinforce what I am saying. I call these sections, "Actions, Not Words." These exercises have been tested many times and will work for most of you. Some of the case histories which I have included may be typical of the average marriage; or they may seem rather extreme to you. But if they don't exactly apply to your situation, just tell yourself, "My marriage isn't in that much trouble. If this advice worked for these people, then maybe there's hope for us."

I am certain that some of my personal biases will come to the surface throughout the remaining chapters. One of these biases is that *sex belongs in marriage*. We can approach this from two different aspects—(1) sex belongs *only* in marriage; (2) sex is a vital part of marriage. I believe both aspects. And the strength for my belief is founded on a very powerful authority.

Recently as I was returning by air from a television show I did in the East, I sat next to an attorney who looked to be near retirement age. With a long flight ahead of us from Norfolk, Virginia through Atlanta, Dallas, Texas and on into Tucson, our conversation drifted to what we did in life. First we talked about his practice as an attorney and his experiences watching the western United States grow to the size and popularity it now is. As the conversation shifted to me and what I had done in life, I told him that I had just returned from doing the "700 Club" with Pat Robertson. After sharing many of my ideas about parenthood and marriage and the need for us to come together as one in marriage, he paused and looked at me inquisitively with, "Young man, where did you ever accumulate so much good common-sense information about how to make a marriage?"

With little hesitation I answered, "Well, to tell you the truth, I got it out of one book." He held up his hand as if to say, "Stop! Don't go any further." Then he reached into his pocket and pulled out a mini calculator-note pad combination and took out his pen. He was now waiting for the name of the book that covered so many vital areas of making a good marriage. I turned to him and said, "Well, it's the Bible, B-I-B-L-E." He nearly dropped his teeth!

That man wasn't the first, nor will he be the last, to learn that the Bible is the best marriage manual ever written. That's what *Sex Begins in the Kitchen* is really premised on, the notion that God created us as man and wife; He sanctified the institution of marriage. He is the one who taught us first that sex belongs *only* in marriage and that sex is a vital part of marriage.

The first book of the Bible tells us that "the Lord God made a woman . . . and he brought her to the man. The man said, 'This is now bone of my bones and flesh of my flesh; she shall be called, "woman," for she was taken out of man.' For this reason a man will leave his father and mother and be united to his wife, and they will become one flesh."[1] This one-ness of flesh is manifested in the sex life between a man and his wife. Paul the apostle went on to explain:

"Do you not know that your bodies are members of Christ himself? Shall I then take the members of Christ and unite them with a prostitute? Never! Do you not know that he who unites himself with a prostitute is one with her in body? For it is said, 'The two will become one flesh.' But he who unites himself with the Lord is one with him in spirit.

"Flee from sexual immorality. All other sins a man commits are outside his body, but he who sins sexually sins against his own body. Do you not know that your body is a temple of the Holy Spirit, who is in you, whom you have received from God? You are not your own; you were bought at a price. Therefore honor God with your own body."[2]

Sex is a vital part of marriage and sex belongs only in marriage. But the sex act must be premised in love between a man and his wife. Marriage Encounter uses a wonderful saying, "Love is a *daily* decision." You can decide when you wake up in the morning if you're going to be loving and happy or grumpy and frumpy. What you do with the love inside you is a daily decision.

If you commit yourselves as man and wife to putting God at the very center of your relationship, and implement many of the ideas I express in *Sex Begins in the Kitchen*, chances are you are going to be richly blessed by a beautiful marriage. It isn't easy. It's not always great. There are low spots as well as highs; but with commitment, each blessing and each drawback can only succeed in bringing greater understanding to your marriage.

Notes
1. See Genesis 2:22-24.
2. 1 Corinthians 6:15-20.

TWO

The Plight of Marriage

The young secretary ripped a piece of paper from her typewriter, crumpled it and threw it in the wastepaper basket. Her supervisor turned to her and asked, "What's wrong with you? Are you in love or something?"

She looked up with a defiant expression on her face and said, "No, of course not! I'm married."

It should surprise no one to learn that the institution of marriage is in a great deal of turmoil and will probably remain under pressure for some time to come. There are, of course, a number of factors that have contributed to marriage being at its present level of decay.

Social Turmoil

The very foundations of marriage have been weakened during the past several decades by a social turmoil, a series of democratic revolutions in our country. There was a time, as you recall, when everyone knew "his place." There was no confusion about our roles; they were carefully spelled out.

Most people assumed that men were *better* than women. We saw whites as being *better* than blacks. Adults, of course, were *better* than children. However, over a several-year period this began to change until today most people view themselves as being of equal worth and value. The kind of society we once lived in where everyone knew "his place" and was too afraid or too meek to speak out against the status quo is obsolete.

The realization that God is no respecter of persons and that He created all mankind—not just men—a little lower than the angels (see Acts 10:34; Ps. 8:5), has brought about a raising of self-esteem in those who were once not included among the *better* people. However, it has also caused those who once looked upon themselves as better to be concerned about their roles in our changing society. As women began to assert themselves and demand equality in the eyes of their husbands and other men, their husbands became confused and insecure, not knowing how to handle this girl who was definitely not "like the girl who married dear old Dad."

These changes have had an adverse affect on marriage and the home and sexual relations. And it's not the change that's bad. The "bad" part was in attitudes we once had about our superior/inferior relationships. Many times, poor sexual relationships between husband and wife are premised on superior/inferior relationships, where somebody is *better* than somebody else. If you go into marriage assuming that you are up here, and your wife is down there somewhere in the pits, I've got news for you: *You're going to lose.* You just can't win in that posture. The fact is that God created us with equal social value. That does not mean that women and men are the same; we are not the same, and I can prove it; it's a little embarrassing but I *can* prove it! The Creator created us distinctly different—we're custom-made for each other in the true sense of the word. But He didn't create one gender superior or inferior to the other.

We live in Tucson, Arizona in the foothills of the desert. We frequently see quail that run up from the wash and into our backyard. One morning I was sitting at the table with my wife, having a cup of coffee. I watched Mom and Dad quail with several little baby quail. The little ones darted around all over the place while Mom quail sort of ran around in circles, kind of like a sheep dog, keeping the little ones together. The old man got up on the birdbath. His contribution was to take a little drink of water and sit there looking around. Meanwhile, there was old Ma, down on her hands and knees, so to speak, with the kids. The thought came to mind: How typical! Here was Father Quail asserting his superior posture, sitting up there drinking, while the poor little woman was down with the children trying to keep them in line. Then it hit me. What he was really doing was living out his role within the family. His role demanded that he seek higher ground so that he could see any danger that may be in the area—maybe a cat that might come and clean up the family for an evening meal. He was *supposed* to watch for any threat to his family and warn them or create a diversion while they escaped.

We assume different roles in our families, and those roles are sometimes subject to change as we go through life. The recent social upheaval in our society has contributed to the turmoil in our marriages. It should have improved marital relationships, but neither husbands nor wives knew how to handle the change in traditional positions.

Inadequate Models

Another factor that has contributed to the plight of modern marriage is that we have never been given adequate models to follow; many of us do not know what an ideal marriage is because we never saw one. In the past several years marriage has degraded almost to the point of no return. I recall a young man who had been married only 13 years. Ron told me one evening, "Doc, I'm telling you, I've been a good husband. I bet I haven't had more than eight other women in those 13 years."

The tragedy of this was that Ron was really serious. He thought he was being a good husband and father; he thought he was being relatively faithful to his wife. What kind of a role was he modeling for his children?

Speaking of modeling, one day I was driving down a city street and had my two-year-old son Kevey with me. He was standing on the front seat next to me when I rolled down the window to—of all things—spit. I had no sooner spit out the window when I caught one on the side of my neck from my two-year-old. Who says that children don't model our behavior?

Unfortunately many of us grew up in homes where there was no loving relationship between our mom and dad. We know that the social learning which takes place in the first few years of the youngster's life is all important. If the model of a loving relationship between the husband and wife is not found in the home, it is very difficult for the child to leave the nest with the feeling that marriage is a loving institution.

One sad truth is that too many of us, in marriage, use each other. We treat each other as objects. Women use men as providers, as escorts, as disciplinarians. Men use women, making them feel like sexual receptacles, like objects. Maybe Mom was held in a subservient position. The young person in the family never saw a caring, loving father who met the needs of his wife and children on a daily basis, only that Dad dumped on Mom. Therefore, when he goes out to seek a permanent relationship with a woman, he will probably deduce that women are for using, and he will select someone whom he can use. Or the young woman may feel that the only role she can perform satisfactorily is the role of mother and homemaker, because her mother taught her that women are only acceptable in this situation. If the young woman has her needs fulfilled in the wife/mother role, that's wonderful. But any aspirations she might have for an additional career or service, or ministry outside the home ought to be encouraged.

It's no secret that children learn about themselves and others from watching, observing and incorporating many of the attitudes, attributes and values that are expressed in the husband/wife relationship within the home. At age six or seven it's a safe guess that the child has an introduction into what the opposite sex is all about. What chance is there for a young male, who has grown up in a home where Mom was used, to ever become a loving, patient, gentle husband, lover, friend? The fact is that without some reeducation he's not going to be any different from his non-caring parent.

Recently I saw a monkey that was allowed out of the cage and taken to a nearby pasture and filmed. Every couple of feet the monkey would thrust his body forward as if to jump from bar to bar. He was demonstrating learned behavior that he had incorporated over the past 15 years. The behavior was so ingrained in the monkey's life that it was difficult for him to behave in any other way. Changing his environment didn't change his personality. We are very much like monkeys. Just because we grow up it doesn't mean that negative behavior will cease. The behavior is usually so ingrained that it follows us into adulthood. Chances are the basic behavior we once exhibited, we still use.

Picture these two situations. Dad comes home from a busy day at the office. Mom's in the kitchen (sex begins in the kitchen?). He comes up and pats her on the "popo" and grabs her to embrace her. Though she doesn't say anything, she struggles loose and turns and glares in such a way that says, *"The children are watching!"*

Now in another home, Dad comes home from a busy day at the office. Mom's in the kitchen. He comes up and pats her on the "popo." But this time Mom turns around and embraces him and gives him a big warm kiss. Sure enough, little Buford and little Festus are watching. Life is a little like the Fram Oil Filter ads—"You can pay me now or pay me later." But you will eventually have to pay. Kids are going to learn things in a positive, OK way or in a negative way. What do you choose for your family? What did your parents choose for you?

Somewhere along the line you may have learned from your parents' example that kissing is bad, hugging is bad, caressing is bad, and since sex was never talked about, it must really be horrendous.

We virtually have no training for the jobs of marriage and parenthood, which is totally tragic. I think that when you are at your worst you are probably being just like your mother or father when they were at their worst. Perhaps our parents were able to keep their marriages together in spite of their problems—partly because of the aversion they may have had to divorce. But in our less restrictive society, and because of the increased pressures and demands we have in our modern surroundings, we cannot keep our marriages together without a meaningful precedent and without some outside help.

We are just beginning to scratch the surface with marriage and parenting education in public schools, churches, through marriage enrichment and Marriage Encounter, parent study groups and seminars sponsored mainly through churches and schools. But there is help available. If you seek help now for your own marriage, and try to model an ideal marriage before your children, the whole complexion of marriage and the home is bound to change in the future.

Maybe you have decided to seek professional help for your marriage. If you and your mate have a communication problem, a physical or sexual problem, or whatever, and you feel a professional opinion and consultation might be worthwhile, begin to look for a professional counselor who wants to get rid of you! Somebody who wants to deal with whatever you present, give you some direction and give you some alternatives on a short-term basis. Don't get locked into a long-term therapeutic marathon. It costs a lot of money for private, individual help; and if the therapist is worth much he will be able to deal with you on a short-term basis—as few as 10 sessions or as many as 20 sessions. When you begin to talk about 60,70,80,90 sessions over a period of years, you wonder if the therapist is really interested in getting the couple on the right road.

To find a qualified counselor start calling people, perhaps from the Yellow Pages. Ask your pastor whom he might recommend. Look for someone who appears to know what he/she is doing, who is well recommended and credentialed in the state as a psychologist or a marriage and family counselor. After getting the names of three or four recommended people, take the time to call them and ask them some questions, the least of which in terms of importance is "How much do you charge?" You aren't looking for the best price for a lawn sprinkler at your local K-Mart. You are talking about someone who is going to enter your very private world, a world which is in an area that is so very vital to your being. Just be sure you find someone who is interested in helping solve your problems quickly and efficiently. Following are some of the other questions you should ask:

1. Do you have spiritual values in your own life?

2. Are you married? How long? How many times?

3. What counseling methods do you employ? Directive or non-directive techniques? Is there one particular model you adhere to?

4. Do you see couples together/individually or some of each? Do you ever see the entire family?

5. How long should we expect therapy to continue? How many sessions, roughly?

6. Will my medical insurance pay for your services? (This question should be directed to your insurance provider as well.)

7. What academic degree(s) do you have? Any postgraduate training?

8. Do you have children? If so, what are their ages?

9. What are your fees? How many minutes in a session? Do you use double sessions? (Sometimes double sessions are desirous, especially if you travel some distance to the place of the appointment.)

10. Can I make monthly payments on my account? What interest rate on the unpaid balance? (Many professionals have gone to a finance charge on the unpaid balance after 90 days.)

11. Are you certified by the State Board of Psychologist Examiners, or other appropriate boards? What are your "professional affiliations"?

Many Christians seek out only Christian professionals. In my opinion it's more important to find a counselor who is competent and able to help you and your mate.

Too-Early Marriages

Besides our social revolution, and the fact that few of us ever had good marriage modeling to follow, our ailing marital situation is suffering from too-early marriages. The number of young people who marry prior to age 20 is astoundingly high.

These young people do not have a realistic view of the responsibilities that go along with marriage and parenthood. Most of them have never seen a good marriage, and the only model they have encountered is the Hollywood glamorous bell-ringing experience they are deluged with. Motion pictures, television, books and advertisements give young people an unrealistic view of marriage.

Whenever I talk to high school students, I tell them that marriage is not all roses. I tell them to picture themselves holding their wives while she is vomiting with the flu over the toilet. Or to see themselves staying home night after night, and awake hour after hour, with a crying baby suffering with diarrhea. Or to realize that they will suffer economic deprivation if they have not taken time to adequately prepare to support a family in the manner they have been used to.

It is too easy for parents to give in to unrelenting demands their teenagers or preteenagers make on them to date. Parents know fully well that the immature teenager would be unable to cope or handle a demanding situation. It isn't easy to consider the implication of too-early dating on your child when he or she is pleading, "*Everybody* I know is allowed to date!"

 The best way to discourage too-early dating is to never encourage it. People frequently ask very young children, in a joking way, "Got a girlfriend yet?" Naturally, the child begins to assume this is something that is expected of him. If it is understood from the time your child is young that he or she can begin dating when he/she reaches the age of 16 (or whatever), then he/she already knows the house rules long before the teen years.

Another thing we as parents do is to make home life so miserable for the teenager that any situation looks rosier than the one he or she is in at the present. Any outreach of "love" is grabbed at without thinking through the consequences.

Denise and Marty, ages 21 and 22 respectively, serve as a case in point. Marty was brought up in a permissive home where he was given far too many freedoms as a young kid, with very few responsibilities. Denise, on the other hand, grew up in a home where there was a very poor marriage. Just about the time she met Marty her parents had gone through a very rough divorce. Not only that but Denise's father had been abusive to her.

At 14 Denise met and began to date Marty, who was 15. It wasn't long before Marty and Denise found themselves in a very intimate relationship. They certainly didn't love each other but at ages 14 and 15 they weren't old enough to know the difference between love and physical infatuation. The lack of male attention and love in Denise's home was a factor that led her to a premature marriage. At 16 she was married, dropped out of school and went to work as a cashier at a grocery store. Her young husband took a job as a carpenter's apprentice. Their marriage somehow survived for five years. They had one daughter. Their marriage was pitifully void of love and it finally became evident that their union was destructive. Now at ages 22 and 21 they were beginning to look around and wonder why their lives were in shambles at such an early age.

Many young couples, as an alternative to marriage, are turning to "living-in" arrangements. I am seeing an increasing number of young couples under 25 who have lived together for one to three years and finally have gotten married. After marriage everything went to pot quickly. Why? Because when they are asked to make a real commitment to someone, they have trouble doing it. Even though a couple has been living together, without being legally married, they really never take off the masks of artificiality with each other. They are still only dating each other on a very intimate basis. They realize that it's important to keep their best foot forward all the time. But when they marry, the "masks" come off, they can relax and be themselves, and trouble soon follows.

I guess we really can't fault the logic that prevails in many young people's minds that says the way to test the waters of married life is to try it out, to live together and see if it's going to work. However, that's a little bit like learning to play basketball by playing badminton; the two are really unrelated. The cohabitation approach is destined for failure. There is a tremendous difference between "living in" and marriage. That's a fact. Yet young people—and some not so young—continue to be duped into thinking that this is a realistic way to test their compatibility for marriage. It's difficult to think "ours" when we are living "mine" and "yours."

You can't blame them too much, because they look at us, the older generation, and often see that their folks haven't done too well in traditional marriages either.

Someone said that only fools say "never"; but here goes anyway. If marriage is not the most important priority in your life, you are *never* going to have a real marriage, a marriage that includes commitment, that is full and satisfying emotionally, sexually, and spiritually. A live-in situation is a commitment, but it's a commitment *not to make a full commitment!* Women I have counseled who have lived with lovers all seem to share a common complaint: They feel cheated that their lovers didn't marry them. They feel that they lost their mates because they lived together with them instead of opting for a traditional marriage. They realize too late that the live-in arrangement has very little to offer them.

Lack of Basic Values

A very major reason why marriage is no longer the strong institution we once felt it was, is that we have strayed from our basic Judeo-Christian values on which our country was formed. We say, "In God We Trust" on our coinage, but we don't show it in our actions. If you believe as I do, that God created us and that man is a spiritual being, how can we expect man to survive if he isn't in touch with his Maker, if he doesn't develop a spiritual life with the Almighty?

There is a lot of meaning in the motto, "The family that prays together, stays together." This may seem like a very simplistic solution to something as complex as marriage, but it works better than any other answer we encounter in our world today. In his book, *Creative Christian Marriage*, author Mark Lee says: "There is in creative Christian marriage a quality of awe and morality. This grows out of spiritual perceptions. Life in humanity is awesome. When it is guided by the morality of God as revealed in the Scriptures, there follows a family beauty that borders on devotion. And when husband and wife, with child, recognize that truth, rising to it, they know there are possibilities that are seldom even hinted at in the literature of marriage. It may have been this insight that caused Martin Luther to say, 'Marriage compels us to believe.'"[1]

There are other reasons why marriage is in so much trouble today. I won't go into them in depth now because I talk about them at length in other chapters, but just to mention a couple. First, *we have never learned to communicate our feelings.* Poor marriages almost always suffer from little or no communication between couples. A deplorable statistic is that couples spend 20 minutes a week in conversation. No wonder we don't have a satisfying and happy relationship.

Another reason why marriage is failing is that *people try to prove to themselves that they are not worth loving.* It is true that many of us have such a low self-esteem and self-concept that we seek out a mate who will reinforce that negative concept within ourselves. That may sound crazy, but, let's face it, human beings are not always rational.

Many of us, in our marriage vows, promise to stay together "for better or for worse." Yet sometimes when things get "worse" we don't hang in there. We don't try to work out our problems. Perhaps only one of you is willing to work at it, but that's a beginning. At the close of one of the seminars I was teaching in, someone handed me the following which illustrates to me that one person, with the right help, is able to turn a marriage around.

"One night I had a dream—I dreamed I was walking along the beach with the Lord, and across the sky flashed scenes from my life. For each scene I noticed two sets of footprints in the sand; one belonged to me, the other to the Lord.

"When the last scene of my life flashed before us I looked back at the footprints in the sand. I noticed that many times along the path of my life, there was only one set of footprints. I also noticed that it happened at the very lowest and saddest times in my life. I questioned the Lord about it. 'Lord, you said that once I decided to follow you, you would walk with me all the way, but I have noticed that during the most troublesome times in my life, there is only one set of footprints. I don't understand why in times when I needed you most, you would leave.'

"The Lord replied, 'My precious child, I would never leave you during your times of trial and suffering. When you see only one set of footprints, it was then that I carried you.'"[2]

Notes
1. Mark Lee, *Creative Christian Marriage* (Ventura, CA: Regal Books, 1977), p. 47.
2. Author unknown.

THREE

Who Did You Marry?

Just a couple of months after I went into private practice a woman called to make an appointment for her son and daughter-in-law. Being somewhat naive at the time I didn't think a great deal of that; but when I began to consult with the young couple I was shocked. In seven months of marriage, Tom and Johanna had never consummated their marital vows! They had never had sex. Not once!

The interesting thing was that Tom and Johanna were both perfectionists and perfectionists are usually found at the top of the family, or first-born children. Tom and Johanna were not first-born children but were the babies of their families; however, they were babies who had several years separating themselves from their older siblings. As such, they were experts in taking from others and very poor at giving. So they were both waiting for the other one to take the first step.

Talk about perfectionists and people who are afraid of failure, this couple took the cake. They were a little like the two kids in the school yard (with adult protection and supervision nearby) who are about to fight. One kid says to the other, "OK, you start it!" The other kid retorts, "No, you start it!" Well, they never started it.

I must admit that Tom and Johanna were one couple I never got to first base with. I should have known that this was going to be an atypical case—the clue was that Tom's *mom* made the appointment. Neither Tom nor Johanna was able to initiate the move. Even with counseling they were unable to make a commitment to each other, much less to me. After they had missed three scheduled appointments, I finally wrote them a letter referring them to someone else in town; I could no longer be in a position where I could service them. Two weeks later their names appeared in the paper as petitioning for divorce. You cannot make another person do anything he or she doesn't want to do.

Tom and Johanna both had personality characteristics of first-born children. When I think of two first-born children who eventually marry each other I envision two rams on a mountainside, butting heads, each one trying to impose its will on the other, for they both know they are right. Competition is fast and furious!

Perhaps you have never taken time to consider this aspect of behavior, but chances are you can learn a lot about your mate, your own self, and your relationship with each other by realizing that your birth order plays a significant role in the development of your personality.

Did you ever stop to consider how very different each of your brothers and sisters is? If you had a serious, intellectual, scholarly, achieving brother or sister in your family, chances are that child was a first-born. If in the same household there was a rough-and-tumble aggressive child, who tended to be impatient and competitive, that brother or sister was probably a middle child. What about the one who got away with murder? The one who screamed from one end of the house, "Hey, Mom, where's my basketball?" The one least likely to be spanked or disciplined by his parent? The one whose nickname was carried on into adult life? Yes, you've guessed it! We're talking about the baby in the family.

The First-Born Child

Remember the day your own first-born came into the world? Special, wasn't it? It was probably the most exciting day in your life! Most of us admit that we place some of our unfulfilled dreams and expectations on that first-born child. In essence we hope the first-born is going to be someone we couldn't be in our own life—like a famous pianist, doctor, lawyer, ballerina . . .

First-borns are in a precarious position of sorts because they have tremendous pressures on them to perform. In most cases they do quite well. As evidence for this phenomenon, I offer the fact that of the first 23 astronauts into space, 21 were first-born children. Many vocations seem to draw the oldest child in disproportionate numbers. Accountants, engineers, computer programmers, architects and doctors tend to be first-born children. Persons who have established themselves in literary and scientific fields are generally first-borns.

Since a first-born's parents are obviously novices at being parents they may overreact to their first-born child;

they often over-parent him, overprotect him. If you think back to the first few days your first-born was home from the hospital, you might recall hearing the baby cough or move. You jumped out of bed immediately to see how the little one was doing. A first-born's parents have a tendency to be very inconsistent. First-borns pay for this experimentation; they become somewhat fearful and apprehensive in their lives. They have a high need not to be criticized. The classic example is when the child knows the answer to the question the teacher is asking but is afraid to put his hand up for fear he might be wrong.

Although there is pressure on first-borns, they are also in a very enviable position in that they have Mom and Dad to themselves for a set period of time. Research tells us that first-born children tend to walk and talk sooner than later children. If the first-born child is also the first grandchild in the family it makes that child's birth all the more special.

First-borns tend to be very much tuned into adult values and feel more comfortable in their presence. They are the ones who enjoy adult conversation and are offended when they are excluded from adult activities. They tend to be dependent upon the family—meaning that first-borns are going to take the family values forward into adult life.

First-borns are achievers; they are reliable, conscientious, apprehensive and conservative. And they are also likely to be perfectionists, a characteristic that is sometimes detrimental to them. Are you a first-born, or are you married to a first-born? What kinds of problems could you be having in your family that could be directly attributed to birth order?

Let me share with you the case of Karin and Jack as found in my first book, *Parenthood Without Hassles* (*Well, Almost)*. Karin was a perfectionist.

"When I think of perfection, I frequently think of a couple I worked with a few years ago—two of the most contrasting personalities I have ever had the occasion to work with. Karin, age 36, was very much a perfectionist and a super mother of six children. She was able to keep her home in perfect order; everything about her, including her children, was as nearly perfect as could be. Physically, she looked like she could have stepped right off the front cover of *Glamour* Magazine: every hair in place and very nattily dressed, she reeked of perfection.

"Jack, on the other hand, looked like he stepped off the cover of *Outdoor Life*. He could have passed as a sheepherder without much difficulty. Their marriage was a very, very competitive one. Karin would push forward and Jack would pull back or retreat. I really had a very difficult time with this young couple, getting them to see that they were in needless competition. The competition had to stop if their marriage was going to make it."[1]

Whenever Karin made a cake for her family she would always make it from scratch—no boxed cake mixes for her! When she had people over for dinner, everything had to be color-coordinated, everything had to be perfect: The napkins matched the plates; there were *fresh* flowers and candles on the table (artificial flowers were a travesty!); the davenport was ironed; the kids were shiny and tidy. The clear vinyl runner which usually greeted people at the door was removed for special occasions only. Guests were actually allowed to walk on the rug!

Karin told me one evening with a sigh of relief, "Dr. Leman, my life changed when I reached for the Ragú Spaghetti Sauce." As with everything else, Karin had made her spaghetti sauce from scratch. Lo and behold, the kids and her husband liked the Ragú Spaghetti Sauce better than they did the start-from-scratch kind!

Karin began to see that she had imposed such high standards for herself that her standards frustrated her and inevitably led to her failure.

I spent a great deal of time in individual therapy with Karin; she began to see that her life was a series of road-blocks, hurdles that she put before herself, which pretty much insured failure. She had expectations for herself and for her husband that were almost unattainable, but they provided her with the opportunity of saying, "Jack, you've fallen short. You haven't measured up. You're no good and I don't like it." Karin had to start someplace in turning around a life-style that was totally engrossed in perfectionism—even in her spiritual life.

Karin was a very fine Christian woman but her relationship with God had to be perfect, and because there aren't many things in life that are perfect she felt very defeated in her spiritual relationship with God. She even felt, subconsciously, that God wasn't perfect; He wasn't big enough to love her, to forgive her for her transgressions.

Finally, Karin made the necessary commitments to begin to change things in her life. She knew it would not come about overnight but she was willing to put forth the effort and the time it would take to make changes. I'm glad to say that Karin and Jack are a couple who made it. They turned the corner. They have developed a relationship that isn't based on competition, on putting the other person down and imposing their own will on the other. To get to that point in life they both had to realize that they were imperfect, that they never could attain that mythical perfection in life. Please don't get the idea that their life is Cinderella-like, that they glided from the old life to a new one. Every day they have to make the decision to defeat the perfection in their lives, to accept each other just as they are. Developing a sense of *imperfection* in their lives is what's going to keep them a happy, sharing, married couple.

Action, Not Words

One of the activities I suggested to Jack and Karin I now share with you. Each day take some time to hold each other and be thankful for the life you have together, for some of the things in life you sometimes take for granted, such as good health, your children, and even some of the amenities life has to offer you. Jack and Karin made a commitment to share feelings with each other every day. You and your mate can make the same commitment. Such a commitment will keep you enjoying a deeper, more loving, happier marriage on a day-to-day basis.

Of course, the ideal for Jack and Karin would have been to get away for a weekend together occasionally, without their six children. But that was very difficult. Even a few minutes a day exclusively for each other was not easy; but it was necessary, and it paid off.

The Second-Born, or Middle Child

To dramatize the plight of the second-born child of a family, I usually ask the parents about the family photo album. Usually they laugh, and rightfully so. Notice the 10,000 pictures of the first-born, bound in 14 volumes? Now compare that to the 19 pictures of the second-born who is always accompanied by his older brother or sister.

Second-born children certainly do have some advantages over the first-born. First of all, they have someone who has plowed the roads of life for them. They have an instant playmate and, more importantly, they have a model. Now if the "model" first child is very temperamental, throws temper tantrums, doesn't do what Mommy and Daddy ask, chances are the second-born is going to go out of his way to become more agreeable, more pleasing to Mom and Dad (especially if second-born is the same sex as first-born).

By the same token, if the first-born becomes a scholar who is reading at age three and brings home straight A's in elementary school, we can expect the second child to seek notoriety in some way other than academically. Think of a tree sprouting and branching off in various directions; so it is with children in the family. It's safe to say that children really have a need to develop differently from their siblings. The theory says that once the first-born grows, develops and assumes a role in the family, that role is rarely challenged by children who follow.

Middle children are sometimes the "black sheep" of the family. They tend to be impatient, aggressive, rebellious and very competitive. In fact, they seem to thrive on competition and tend to be much more independent than first-born children. But we also think of middle children as the mediators, the peacemakers, and very social. Since they are outgoing they have many satisfying friendships. They want the seas of life to be smooth. They are often called upon to solve sticky situations with other members of the family.

Susan and John had been married for 17 years when

they called for an appointment. They were both middle children. The thing I remember most was that they were at a point where their kids were entering the teenage years and they were beginning to look down the road to the day when the children would be gone and they would be by themselves once again (avoiding a possible sticky situation?). They had a good, solid marriage but they felt they needed some reassurance and guidelines which would make their good marriage even better. I believe their characteristic of being mediators in life helped their marriage become a good, positive union of two people. They admitted to having some spats and disagreements, like most couples, but through the process of negotiation they were able to sit down and face things squarely on.

Middle children tend to take life in stride, let undue stress roll off their backs like oil. Yet they are tenacious enough that when a problem comes along they want to dig in and get it settled. They don't like troubled waters. A marriage involving a middle child is often very positive.

The Youngest Child

The youngest child in the family, as I mentioned earlier, tends to be the person most likely to get away with murder; he is the least likely to be spanked, punished or pummeled. Youngest children seem to be helpless, manipulative, charming, social, independent, demanding and very good at putting others at their service. Youngest children are special in that their birth marks the end of the trail, so to speak. Youngest children are also in a very special position having older brothers and sisters to model after, from whom they can assimilate personality skills and traits.

The youngest, being physically the smallest, is very good at setting up old Mom and Dad. When you hear the royal battle between the children it's usually the youngest who has subtly set up the situation. He's very good at egging his siblings on, yelling the loudest; he enjoys his parents' wrath upon brother or sister which he so skillfully has set up.

When I think of a marriage that involves a baby in the family I can't help but think of my own. As the youngest of three children who got away with far too many things in life, I really thought that God sent my wife special delivery to me, to meet all my needs. After we returned home from our honeymoon we lived in a men's residence hall with 360 men on the University of Arizona campus. We were so naive at the time that we didn't realize that this was a demanding way to start the marriage; but we had very few problems adjusting to the new environment.

Things went amazingly smooth. I came home at night and took off my clothes. I then proceeded to drop them down over chairs and the all-convenient floor. My wife, being a first-born with a compulsion to be neat, went around and picked up after me. I thought that was an absolutely great relationship. I'd throw my clothes down and she would pick them up just like my mother had done for me my first 23 years. It was only after hearing me talk at some of my presentations to parent groups on the theme of accountability training, that she got the idea that *her* husband needed some "training."

Things got progressively messier in the apartment and I guess I didn't think a great deal of it until one day I came home and tried to push open the front door. It was very difficult due to the clothes piled a foot deep on the floor! My poor wife! In exasperation, after failing to get my attention by refusing to pick up after me, she pulled all the clothes out of the drawers and threw them all over the house. I finally caught on (yes, some babies are slow learners). She was no longer going to be my mother, she wanted to be my wife. I must admit, I still throw things down once in a while but I'm a lot better than I was early in my marriage.

So, if you are married to a baby, take a look at his family. What is his relationship with his mother and father? You can probably get a pretty good idea about some of the work that you might have to do as husband or wife with a "baby" for a spouse. Unfortunately too many men grow up believing that a wife is a personal maid. So when his wife is sick he has no idea how to do a load of wash or make her some hot tea. This is really a tragedy!

If your wife was a special princess in the family who got a lot of attention, then as a husband you better be attentive or she will be very disillusioned in her marriage.

The Only Child

The *only child* tends to be first-born in triplicate! Most of the characteristics associated with first-borns apply to the "lonely onlys" as well. The difference is that they become super-reliable, super-conscientious. They tend to impose very high standards on themselves which is carried over into marriage and parenthood. One of the difficulties only children have is the inability to get along with their peers in their childhood. They prefer adults, as they have been the biggest influencing factor in their lives. *Only children* often marry people who are several years older or younger than themselves.

You might be asking yourself at this point, "Why is the author taking me into a mini course in child psychology?" I'll tell you why. *The little boy or girl you once were, you still are.* And, in order to understand why we develop so uniquely different, why we seem to have trouble getting to know our husband or wife, we must have an understanding of personality characteristics of the different birth orders.

Do you think, now that you are married, that you are different from how you were in your family? We find that the only little girl in a family who was a pampered princess, the apple of her daddy's eye, is going to expect her husband to treat her in the same fashion. If her husband doesn't measure up to the kind of treatment she expects (the measuring stick is her daddy), their marriage has a problem.

Action, Not Words

Who did you marry? A good exercise for you and your mate is to spend some time behind closed doors talking about your respective families. Find out how your husband or wife (or boyfriend/girlfriend) felt about their brothers, sisters, and their dad and mother. Then try to determine what roles were acted out within the family unit. Who was the black sheep? Who was the mediator? Who was the manipulator? We tend to marry people outside of our birth order. First-borns tend to marry babies, and babies tend to marry first-borns or middle children.

Often, though, we see two perfectionists marry, or two babies. When these people marry we sometimes see some very stormy and interesting marriages (for example, Tom and Johanna).

Once you have discovered that you have married the pampered princess in the family or the baby in the family (the instant wonder of the world) the first thing you have to come to grips with is that *you can't change that person.* There is no way you are going to change the leopard's spots. But you can change your own behavior in such a way so that you don't allow the perfectionistic standards to be a menace to yourself. In other words, you can allow your husband to have extremely high expectations for himself but it is very unfair for him to make those expectations of you or your children. The only way you are going to get away from those kinds of things is to make it clear that you have no intention of changing him but that you're going to change your own behavior. Then we *allow* our mate to change his or her behavior, because he or she *wants* to change.

In the case where you discover you have married a man who has been pampered, where his mother did everything for him, a good honest communication session behind closed doors is best. "Hey! Listen! I'm not your mom, I don't want to be your mom, I am your wife. I want to treat you like my husband, I want you to treat me like your wife." Allowing him to throw his clothes around the house would not be an act of love. Marriage does bring mutual responsibilities. When you expect someone to pick up after you you are essentially being very disrespectful. If your wife is "too tired" every night you might look around the house and see if you're demanding her to be more of a maid than a mate.

Usually when we do alter our own behavior, we begin to see changes in the behavior of others. This is often demonstrated in family therapy. When the little "black sheep" who came for therapy begins to turn around, the little super brother or sister—who is one year older or younger—begins to act in a negative manner. Why? Because as people, we really interact with one another as a dynamic entity, meaning that one of the reasons why the black sheep is the bad guy in the family is that older brother Harold is so perfect. So when the black sheep begins to take on more positive behavior, it is really a threat to Harold and he doesn't know how to handle it. He now has a brother who is behaving differently from what he trained him to be.

So be brave and start to alter your own behavior. You can't row another person's canoe.

Exceptions to the Rule

Have you seen yourself in any of the foregoing descriptions, or your mate? If not, maybe your situation comes under the category of "Exceptions." There are many variables that affect the personality characteristics. For example, if your oldest brother is physically handicapped, although you are going to see yourself as a second child, you actually will develop characteristics of a first-born.

The sex of the child may be a variable. If the first two children of the family are the same sex they are usually opposite in personality. If the first two children are of different sex there is the possibility that they will both reflect the characteristics of first-born children, depending upon how traditional the family is. The family may have very separate expectations for the first-born male and the first-born female in the same family, so sex is an important variable.

In a family of three older girls and one baby boy, you don't have to be a psychologist to figure out that the first-born and only boy weighs very special in the family. If any of the children tends to be the "black sheep" it would be the third-born girl. Having a "king" born right after her could impair her self-esteem and take away her specialness.

The years between the birth of each child is a variable that affects personality characteristics of children. If there is a five- or six-year gap between the births of the children, I would say you essentially have two first-borns. So it is possible, particularly in a large family, to have two or more children with first-born tendencies.

As I mentioned at the beginning of this section, *a third variable that affects personality characteristics in children is a physical handicap.* Any child who has a physical handicap becomes "special" no matter where he is born in the family. So much depends on how the parents treat that handicapped child. If the child is slightly handicapped and a sibling is born within a year or two, there is a good chance that the two children would have a role reversal, the sibling child actually takes over and assumes the leadership role in the family as a first-born.

Sometimes there will be a role reversal if children are drastically different. For example, if the first child is of slight build but the second child is a moose, there is a good probability that the second child, or "Moose," would take on first-born qualities. In this case the first-born child could feel very defeated in life because of the second-born hulk of a boy.

A miscarriage or death of a child is a variable that has a great impact on the whole family, but the greatest impact is felt by the child directly following each incident.

The last variable I am going to mention is the *parents' interaction with the individual children.* In a typical family various roles will be assumed by different children: there might be the achiever, scholar, perfectionistic first-born, the comedian second child, the athlete third, the artistic or musical or, possibly, black sheep fourth child. We can usually predict the role each person will assume in that family. Once a role is assumed it is rarely challenged; there is not enough uniqueness in being the same as your brother and sister, you want to be different. Also you'll find a lot of resentment when a sibling tries to steal someone else's "thunder."

You will find families where all are athletic, scholarly or musical and there is no rivalry. Parents have dealt with their children in a noncompetitive way. They take for granted that they will all participate in a particular family value, and it really isn't important that you are not good at that particular value. What's important is that everyone participates, and the stress of winning or losing is nonexistent.

This has all been said to help you realize how important it is for you to understand how you and your mate developed a series of personality traits. These personality traits are really logical, in spite of the fact that you may feel that your mate does something just to irritate you.

Action, Not Words

Take time to diagram your own family, the family your mate grew up in and the family where you are now parents. Beside the name of each person use an adjective to describe him or her. Then see what conclusions you can draw from the diagrams. Can you see reasons why you and your mate developed the way you have? Can you see how you are helping your children develop in the way they are? Remember, the little boy or girl you once were, you basically still are.

Your diagram might look something like this:

Husband's family

Festus (husband), 41	Perfectionist, reliable accountant
Harold (brother) 39	Easy-going, artistic
Buford (brother) 38	Charming, salesman
Beatrice (sister) 35	Manipulative, demanding

Wife's family

Sally (sister) 45	Bookkeeper, temperamental
Samantha (sister) 43	Independent, competitive, career woman
Sissy (wife) 39	Easy-going, helpless, homemaker

Our family

Dad, Festus	*Mom, Sissy*
Phineus 13	Scholarly, apprehensive
Harold 12	Rebellious, sloppy, athletic
Princess 9	Independent, cute, demanding
Moose 3	Spoiled (rotten), strong-willed, precocious

Can you guess why Festus and Sissy were drawn together in marriage?

Note
1. Kevin Leman, *Parenthood Without Hassles* (*Well, Almost)* (Eugene, OR: Harvest House Publishers, 1979), pp. 25-27. Used by permission.

FOUR

Making the Pieces Fit

A s we showed in the previous chapter, we really haven't changed much since we were kids. In "Who Did You Marry?" we talked about how our birth order can affect the kind of person each of us is and how it influences our marriage.

In this chapter we will think about "life-style analysis"—a process by which we go back and put together the pieces to the puzzle of your childhood in order to help you understand how you got where you are today. In other words we're going to take a look at the society which surrounded you as a child—mom, dad, siblings, and possibly other close relatives such as grandparents, those who are generally in your immediate family.

We will meet several personalities—attention-getter, controller, martyr, pleaser, carrot-seeker, cop-out artist, revenger—all real people, all with problems that can hinder them from having successful, fulfilling, happy marriages.

One of the issues psychologists, psychiatrists and mental health people agree on is that our personalities form in the first few years of our lives, generally speaking by the first six or seven years. Like many other things in life, personality traits and characteristics are learned by trial and error. This personality development results in how we behave. Behavior is that which works for us, serves a purpose in our lives, gets us to a desired goal, is reinforced, and eventually ingrained into our daily life, becoming a life-style.

The life-style we established in childhood is very resistant to change. Unless you undergo psychotherapy or are faced with some kind of traumatic experience, or make a concerted effort to change your ways, or experience a spiritual renewal, we can be pretty sure that the behavior you displayed as a youngster you will probably display in your adult life-style many years later.

The Attention-Getter

One of the most common life-styles we see today is the attention-getter. The attention-getter can be found in two positions in the family in disproportionate numbers: in the first-born child or in the baby. The "baby" will usually seek attention on a negative tone while the positive attention-getter is likely to be the oldest.

The first child in the family develops this life-style because so much love and attention was devoted to that first special birth. This is even more pronounced when the first child is also the first grandchild in the family. With so much adult attention paid to every little movement of the child, it doesn't take long for him to learn that he really is the center of attention and that he becomes very good at commanding the attention of others.

For example, take a 12-month-old who is sitting in the high chair and, by accident, drops the spoon on the floor. The old man turns to his wife and says, "Boy, oh boy, did you see the arm on that kid! He's going to be another George Brett!"

The child, seeing the adult reaction, will watch Daddy put the spoon back on the high chair and then will throw the spoon again, but this time he giggles and laughs. Dad, still impressed with the "strong arm" of the 12-month-old, continues to smile and laugh, essentially praising the child.

About the thirteenth time little Junior throws the spoon on the floor, Dad becomes somewhat irritated and begins to show interest in keeping the spoon off the floor. But Dad's initial reaction causes baby to deduce in his mind that he can get attention and play very enjoyable games with the adult by this behavior.

Children are very sensitive early in life to the kinds of behavior that command attention. If the child gets attention, even negative attention, for being mischievous there is a high probability that he'll always get attention when he behaves mischievously. If we pay attention to the child at the times he is doing things that are ouside the family guidelines, then we are really reinforcing the unwanted behavior.

The attention-getting life-style will fall into two basic areas: *constructive* and *destructive*. The constructive attention-getter, usually the first-born child in the family, learns to do things very well with close adult supervision and guidance and can become extremely precocious. As soon as he hits preschool or kindergarten, guess what? He tends to do very well! School is one of the initial proving grounds in life. Constructive attention-getters tend to do well academically.

He gets attention by doing the right things, by being coopera- tive in the home, by getting good grades in school and, in general, by being socially acceptable.

The destructive attention-getter, on the other hand, can get attention through negative means, perhaps by always keeping an adult busy with him, always demanding attention by showing off, or being a "pain in the neck" or a "know-it- all." His life-style also begins to develop. From his childish point of view he only counts in life when he can get others' attention, either positively or negatively.

In a social situation with other children, the attention- getter will usually rise to the top very quickly and might do things in the presence of others to command attention. The demand for attention is usually insatiable. The attention- getter usually can't get enough of it. When an adult reacts to a youngster's antics by way of a reprimand, the attention- getting child will usually stop long enough for the adult to get back to his own routine, then negative behavior reappears.

Now what, pray tell, is going to alter the child's deep need to be noticed as he develops into the preadolescent, adoles- cent, teenage years? If the attention-getting is positive, he is going to do well in school, be involved in activities, and have many friends. If he is on a negative track, chances are he is going to become a behavior problem in school, in Sunday School, in the home. He'll be very good at doing things in such a way that he gets constant reminding, coaxing and nagging—attention!

When I think of grown-up attention-getters I think of a young couple I worked with many years ago, Joel and Suzi. As a child, Suzi was the "princess" in her family. She had three older brothers and never lacked for attention in that she was the only girl in the family. The apple of Daddy's eye was very precocious, very demanding, and very good at getting others to notice her. She used charm, her cuteness and her temper to demand attention.

Suzi married Joel, a perfectionist, the oldest child in his family and very responsible. When Joel was nine years old his father died, which made him the "little man" of the house. When he grew up and married, Joel's personality dictated that he always knew what was best for his wife since he was always so reliable and conscientious and perfection-oriented.

Joel was a bicycling enthusiast. His idea of bicycling wasn't to just go out for a little bike ride, it was to go out for a weekend and at least a hundred miles. *He* decided that this would be a great activity that he and Suzi could do together, so he bought his wife a $350 racing bike. (Remember, any time you enter into a social relationship, knowing what's best for the other person, you're likely to head for trouble, and trouble is what Joel got.) His wife, after several futile attempts to keep up with him (he usually rode several miles ahead of her) finally gave up and decided that there would be no more "restful" weekends chasing her husband down busy highways. Did that deter dear old Joel? No way! He still had to put in his miles so that he could feel he was accomplishing something on the weekend.

After several weekends of leaving Suzi at home while he went about his cycling, Joel came home late one Sunday afternoon, exhausted after bicycling all day and plopped himself in front of the TV. Suzi, the baby in her family who only counts in life when she's noticed, was seething. She felt in direct competition with the TV set and the bike. In anger, she went out and attacked Joel's prize bed of tulips. Now, envision a knee-high bed of tulips, 40 feet long and four feet wide, of various colors, all about the same height. Now visualize that sea of tulips with all the flowers lopped off, just the stems sticking skyward like toothpicks! In anger, Suzi chopped off every one of them with trimming shears!

I'm not suggesting that if your mate isn't noticing you that you go out and destroy one of his prized possessions in life. But this is an example of how really compelling is the need some of us have to be noticed. Suzi got Joel's attention! She got it with negative behavior but she got his attention, and *wrath*! In this situation *any* attention was desirable—she just wanted to be noticed.

I made a great deal of headway with Joel and Suzi, but it took understanding on both their parts to really see the driving forces in their lives, Suzi's for attention and Joel's to be a winner, an achiever, to always do well. It took compromise and commitment on both their parts to make sure they met the needs of each other within the marriage. Joel soon learned that every time he put his wife in the position where she was the center of attention, she purred like a kitten. Suzi had to learn to give Joel credit for his achievements, and also some time for himself. Joel had to learn to budget his time more equally; and both of them finally agreed on some set hours when Joel could take off and do his bicycling. There were some times when they actually did bicycle together, but side-by-side, not in race-like fashion.

The Controller

Is your mate shy? Temperamental? Chances are that if he/she exhibits either trait we're talking about the controller. The controlling life-style is a very interesting one and one that is probably the most difficult to deal with within marriage. The controller tends to play his cards very close to his chest. Very rarely does he give you a glimpse of his real self. It's only in very select environments, where there is extreme trust, that the controller will open up and share his real self with others.

The controllers are experts at hiding their feelings. They are great at keeping people at arm's length. When they do search out and find someone they think they can trust, they become very harbor-like, meaning that they have a very narrow passageway into what really makes them tick. To get close, you have to be very careful that you enter the harbor in a very cautious and non-threatening manner. If you become too pushy the harbor might close with little or no notice at all.

The controller often wears two different "masks." We have the controller who controls his life as well as the lives of others because he enjoys pulling all the strings, controlling every situation, being behind the steering wheel of life. Then we have a controller who controls for defensive purposes— he controls his life out of fear that someone else will control it for him. In fact, it is interesting that one of the fears a controller may have is the fear of losing his mind, or the fear of death; when you think of the loss of control, losing one's mind or one's life is the very ultimate.

If you've married a controller, you know what I'm talking about. They are very reticent to open up and share any feelings with you. You can pry, coax, plead, but to no avail. The controller has learned early in life to become turtlelike; a safe posture to assume to keep things under close wraps. If we probe at or around him we can rest assured that the controller will remain under that protective shell which locks out the people who love him most.

When we retreat in such a fashion we are really denying a part of us that makes us a whole human being. All of our feelings—tears, anger, humiliation, and all the rest—combine to make us complete.

Fred and Linda are good examples of a controlling marriage. Fred, age 39, expressed his need to be in control through intellectualizing, through being perfect, and by being hung up on neatness as a virtue in life. Fred was an accountant, a profession where many of his perfectionistic tendencies were met every day in his life's work.

Linda complained that every time she went to cuddle up or talk with Fred, he found something for his busy hands to become engaged in—such as washing the car, mowing the lawn, gardening, or whatever. It seemed almost as if he had a definite plan to avoid contact with his wife. The one exception was the nights when *Fred* desired sex. Then he pursued her in a very methodical, clinical manner, without any consideration or affection for Linda. Linda's reaction to the sexual relationship, as you might imagine, was one of horror. For her, sex began early in the day, but that's when he chose to wash the car rather than talk about their relationship. So when Fred did become attentive, as preparation for sex, Linda felt very used. "I love you," didn't really mean much to her in bed when his actions during the course of the day didn't seem to show it. Therefore, she had no feelings of sexual fulfillment; no climax or orgasm occurred. On the other hand, Fred was very content with his hedonistic sex life. He essentially took from Linda and basically used her.

After several weeks of therapy with Linda, I got her to see that there was no use trying to make Fred something he wasn't. All her pleading, coaxing, reminding hadn't worked in their 13 years of marriage, and it wasn't going to work. Finally I convinced her to begin to act in a totally different manner than she had previously. As she began to back off and give up trying to remake him, Fred realized that something was changing in their relationship. He realized that he no longer controlled Linda and he was very threatened by the fact that she was no longer chasing him. When she stopped chasing him and began to be independent of him he finally began to seek out Linda, asking simple questions like, "What's wrong? Do we need to talk about something?"

Action, Not Words

If you have "preached" for many years in a marriage and tried to get the other person to change, now might be the time to back off and do the unexpected, to change your behavior and see what happens. If your mate tells you to get off his/her case, get out of his/her life, do it! Get out temporarily! The next time your mate asks for something, gently remind him or her *in love* that you are temporarily out of his/her life.

The marital relationship has a crucial balance and when one side changes, the other generally changes in the opposite direction. A couple is an entity in and of itself. Each member depends upon the other's behavior to keep himself in the same relative position. When one position changes, it means that the other will have to change, too.

It was a joy to watch Fred and Linda begin to come together in marriage. But it took determination, hard work and a lot of commitment on Linda's part to stop playing the game; furthermore, it took a lot of retraining and compromising from Fred to get him to a point where he could begin to open up and share. I found that Fred had a deep-seated fear within him that if he told his wife who he really was, how guilt-ridden and inadequate he was inside, she would *reject* him. He felt that a man's role had to be the strong one. His interpretation of sharing feelings was that of weakness. They both told me that the highlight of their 13-year marriage was the night they finally wept in each other's arms. It is still easy for Fred to go back to the learned behavior of shutting people off. He has to consciously think about it and internally commit himself to be open with himself and with others.

Life-style is very ingrained in a person's life. It starts when we are children and continues to be reinforced as we grow, and is very difficult to change. Fred had 39 years of learning to be the person he was. It was not behavior that he could turn around overnight. He had to make that constant decision within himself and say, "Hey! I'm going to be brave, I'm going to be open, I'm going to do some things that are very counter to what my basic personality is all about."

Interestingly, one of Fred's early recollections of childhood is going to a birthday party with several children. He was the last to enter the room and waited, shyly, to be escorted by the mother into the room. By Fred's own admission he was very shy but whenever I see a "shy" person I recognize a person who is indeed powerful and could very well be a controller. Even at age four Fred was capable of making other people come to serve him. He was a controller. He deserved special attention. More importantly, he got it.

I remember several years ago working with a five-year-old girl. She was sitting on the chair talking in a sweet, gentle inaudible voice. I kept leaning over trying to get closer to her, cupping my hand to my ear trying to increase the probability of hearing her. Then all of a sudden it hit me! That little five-year-old had me in the palm of her hand. I could just feel her wheels turning. She was probably thinking, "I wonder if I can get the crazy psychologist off the chair and onto the floor, flat on his face."

Recognizing the controller isn't easy. He is often the person we least suspect as being the controller of others. When he approaches us from a position of shyness, he is saying, "I want to make you pay attention to me. I want to control the situation because I'm special."

Controllers use the skills of temper, tears, shyness, and intellectualizing to keep people at their distance. Controllers tend to operate on the power principle which says, "I only count in life when I control, win, or dominate."

The Martyr

Another common life-style is the martyr. A martyr is frequently found as a marital mate to an alcoholic. Alcoholics essentially need martyrs to walk on and use and abuse in the true sense of the word, and martyrs have the deplorable need to be walked on.

As a youngster, the martyr feels he is not worth loving, and this is reinforced in several different ways. He generally has a very poor relationship with the parent of the opposite sex and gets the idea that he isn't worth loving. He goes out in life and chooses a mate who will reinforce this negative interpretation of himself.

I worked with a martyr, Janet, age 37, who recently had married for a second time. Janet was *agoraphobic* (fearful of being in open spaces). I realized she was a martyr one evening when she explained that she was having such traumatic experiences in supermarkets. She would become panic-stricken to the point where she had to run from the store because she felt that her air supply was cutting off and she was about to faint. I really startled her with a statement. "Janet, I'll bet you anything that your husband is an alcoholic."

She turned to me and said, "Well, he is, but how did you know?" I said, "I didn't know but I guessed because you have just told me that you really are a martyr. You had to run out of the store for fear that *someone else* would see you faint."

What I was hearing is that she wasn't worth the attention she would get if she fainted in the store. Martyrs are very difficult to deal with because they have the need to do themselves in and they put themselves in this unenviable position.

Neither Alice nor Johnny were martyrs, but Alice's mom was, and unfortunately she lived with them. (I say unfortunately because a family should really live by themselves if at all possible. It's difficult enough to make a marriage run smoothly without having someone else to contend with.) Alice's mother was very much a martyr. She was getting up in years and was very good at making Alice and Johnny feel guilty when they left her alone. Therefore, they went out of their way to be sensitive to her needs. It wasn't until therapy, however, that we exposed the tyranny of Mom's martyrdom. It was only after they began to make commitments to take care of themselves, treat their relationship as the most important relationship, that Mom's martyr-like behavior began to decrease. It had lost it's purposive nature.

I think the thing that distresses me so much about martyrs is the fact that so many of them are females and many are Christian women who have assumed that the answer to everything in life revolves around the concept of *love, love, love.* "If I just LOVE my alcoholic husband enough, everything will work out OK." Nothing could be further from the truth. All evidence points to the fact that when the mate of an alcoholic pulls the rug out and makes him stand on his own two feet, then and only then, can the alcoholic go forward and be accountable for his own actions. A martyr husband or wife needs to stop making excuses for the spouse's drinking. It doesn't do any good to hide or pour the liquor down the drain. Remove yourself totally from becoming involved. *You* cannot control the drinking. The best attitude is "I love you but your drinking will have to be *your* responsibility."

Other Christian women I have worked with, who are caught up in the martyr life-style, suffer under the illusion that they are to be submissive to their husbands in all things. I don't believe that's true. I don't believe that God created women to be used or abused in any way, shape or form; yet I have countless examples of women who were forcibly held down for sex, physically beaten, cheated on and degraded tragically, but hung on, thinking that they were acting the way God wanted them to act as wives. There comes a time when you have to love yourself on the basis that the Almighty loves you. You have to take a stand for yourself and get yourself out of a situation that is destructive to you and your family.

Many misinterpret the whole notion of submissiveness in marriage. The Scripture teaches specifically that women are to be submissive to their husbands. On the other hand, the Scripture also teaches husbands to "love your wives as *Christ* loved the church."[1] A husband must love his wife to such an extent that he is willing to lay down his very life for her. Whenever I have the opportunity in a seminar to use the word "submissive," I always do so because there is such a great need to understand that submissiveness means a *mutually submissive* partnership, not just the wife giving and the husband taking, or the reverse.

The martyr who leaves the situation that is causing him to be degraded is often taking the very first positive step that he will ever take in his life. This is a reaffirmation of the fact that he is worth loving. It's very difficult for people who have been stepped on and squashed over a long period of time to get to a point where he gains some notion of self-esteem or self-respect.

I remember one woman whose husband had left her 32 times for another woman—the same woman. What made it more unfortunate was that the wife was 49 years old and the other woman was 65 years old. You can imagine what this situation did to the wife's self-esteem.

Action, Not Words

I gave the jilted wife a very simple assignment. If you feel you need help in reaffirming your self-esteem try this little exercise. Look into a mirror and repeat a very simple prayer, "Lord, help me love myself as I know you love me." Do this day after day until you begin to love yourself.

For that woman the prayer was a source of inspiration and encouragement. Her love for her husband was all-encompassing. Slowly she realized that her feelings were worthy of someone else who would not take advantage of her as her husband did. He was not willing to change. After all, he had his cake and frosting too!

The Pleaser

We meet the pleasers in life daily. You know them! They're the ones who just have to make sure everybody likes them, that everybody approves of everything they do in life. They are extremely sensitive to every kind of criticism. One of the social skills that pleasers develop very early in life is the ability to read up on an issue and flow with the prevalent attitude of almost any discussion between a group of people. They seem to go around in life always having to gain approval. Many attention-getters are into the pleasing life-style.

Often we see life-styles come together and compliment each other. The pleaser can make it in life, but usually not over the long haul; sooner or later it gets pretty wearing to continue pleasing everybody and trying to make everybody like you. That is when most pleasers come to an abrupt halt and begin to ask themselves the question, "What about me? When do *my* needs get pleased? When do *my* needs get met?" I usually give pleasers an assignment where they can stand up and share their real feelings, first of all with themselves and then with someone they are very close to, preferably the husband or wife. Pleasers are afraid that if they speak their own mind, they will be rejected, and therefore unloved.

I've learned to ask certain questions to determine whether or not a person is a "pleaser." I present a hypothetical situation: If you are in a restaurant and you are served a meal which is not to your liking, what do you do with the dinner? Do you return it or do you eat it and wish you had enough gumption to complain? Usually the "pleaser" will eat it because he doesn't want to make waves, and out of guilt he will leave a good-sized tip besides!

My wife and I went out to a very simple first-class restaurant one evening. I don't know what it is about first-class places, but we tend to order things we wouldn't order in other restaurants. I had Long Island duckling and my wife had salmon. When the salmon arrived at the table, it looked like it was still moving upstream! My wife commented that it wasn't quite done but she began eating around the more fully cooked edges. (She admits to being a pleaser!) I thought to myself, "No way am I going to pay for that!" I called the waiter over and told him that the lady's salmon was not done and asked him to return it to the kitchen. He was most apologetic and quickly took her plate away. Moments later the maitre d' came to our table and expressed his sincere apologies. Two minutes later the head waiter came over relaying the chef's apologies and bringing us the news that the chef was preparing a little something for our dessert, compliments of the house, of course, as his way of showing how sorry he was for not having the dinner prepared correctly. Within a few minutes we had the salmon on the table, done to perfection. After dinner the waiter brought us baked Alaska flambé, covered with a pure marshmallow sauce, drenched with fresh strawberries! Now, whenever I go to that restaurant, I call the waiter over and say, "Excuse me, but this meal isn't *exactly* the way my wife ordered it!" (I'm only kidding, but I'd do almost anything for baked Alaska!)

The Carrot-Seeker

Due to our traditional upbringing of reward and punishment, many of us have grown up looking for a reward in everything we do in life. We've done a good job in our traditional society in developing the carrot-seeker life-style. The carrot-seeker simply goes around looking for a carrot at every turn. When he doesn't get praised or reinforced for every little achievement, he is deeply offended and hurt.

Very similar to the pleasing life-style, the carrot-seeker says, "I only count in life when other people notice what I do and reward me for such behavior." Well, there are certain situations in life where I suppose the carrot-seekers can do very well, but basically they run into the same kind of difficulty as the pleaser. Sooner or later, generally later, that kind of life-style becomes very unfulfilling.

When a person has to receive a "thank you" for everything he does, or expects some mention of approval, that person is a carrot-seeker. Eventually he must realize that he does things for others only to serve himself. Jesus said of this type person that he won't be rewarded later, "He already has his reward."[2] If a charitable deed or a courtesy is done in the right vein, no one will be told about it and the person who does it is never acknowledged.

Many times a young homemaker will break her neck to put on a beautiful dinner just for her husband. If her husband isn't observant, alert and encouraging in his remarks about the wonderful dinner he might very well find his wife whimpering behind closed doors because she wasn't given her due reward.

Action, Not Words

If you think you might be a carrot-seeker, why don't you try this assignment which I often give carrot-seekers. Do something for yourself each week, whatever gives you satisfaction. You can take a knitting class, a ceramics class, join an athletic club—any kind of activity outside the home, away from the children, just for self-satisfaction. The reward is that you are doing things which you feel are worthwhile. Time for yourself is essential. The reward comes only from doing something satisfying, and there's lots of good results from treating yourself in an OK fashion. You don't have to have the approval of anyone else, only your own feeling of self-worth and self-esteem is important.

The Cop-Out

The person with the cop-out life-style can generally be found at the very top of the family, or at the other extreme—the youngest of the family. If the person is the oldest, chances are his parents had very high expectations for him. If he is at the bottom of the family, chances are that the children above him were *very* successful, which had a defeating effect upon him, creating a cop-out life-style. Cop-outs tend to be very inadequate people.

Very rarely do you see these people complete any kind of task. It's even abnormal to see them start tasks as they grow older in life. Their mission seems to be to prove to others that they can't do anything efficiently. If something is going to be done in their life, it's going to be done through another person, by someone else's actions.

To help the cop-out artist, people who are close to him must withdraw from the scene, refusing to do anything for him that he can do for himself. In addition, good professional help should be sought to help the cop-out artist.

The Revenger

One of the reasons I am very pessimistic about rehabilitation programs for hard-core criminals and drug addicts is that they have been firmly entrenched in the revengeful life-style. The revengeful life-style basically says that the person feels hurt by life, life has been unfair to him; therefore, he has a right to strike back at life.

Rarely do we see the revengeful life-style develop earlier than age seven or eight. At this age the child learns to be powerful or controlling. It takes time to develop, but the revengeful life-style has a goal in life to hurt other people. The result of their action to themselves is inconsequential. Any hurt they suffer in return only enforces the misconception they hold of life. How else can you explain senseless killing, vandalism and deviancy in our society?

It's not very often that you get a chance to see people in marital therapy who are into revengeful behavior, whose life-style is one of revenge. Marion, age 33, had grown up in a home where the father abused not only Marion, but her mom as well. He finally deserted the family when Marion was six years of age.

Marion, the oldest child, was one of those people who pulled herself up in life by the bootstraps and went forward. She went on and earned good grades in school and ended up with a Master's degree in her profession. She wanted very much to have her own children but was unable to. Finally she and her husband, Roger, settled on adopting a child.

Roger reported that one day he came home from work at the normal time and found the home in disarray and their three-year-old son, Jimmy, black and blue. Roger said that Marion always had a problem with temper and sometimes she would become explosive. He thought that sometimes she was disciplining the child too hard but this was his first realization that his wife was physically abusive toward their son.

You may be asking yourself at this point, How can an adult beat a child to the point of the child being black and blue from head to toe? I really don't know how, but I have some idea as to why. Marion's life-style seemed to reek of the fact that life had been unfair to her, that she had been kicked in the teeth; therefore, in her mind she felt that she had the right to strike out at others. As the first-born child herself, she was a perfectionist. As you can imagine, with a three-year-old in the home things are far from perfect.

Many times when things went wrong within herself she overreacted to the point where she just wanted to do harm to the child. The revengeful life-style is very difficult to deal with because it is so ingrained and so strong. As I said, the criminal element in our society usually exhibits revengeful kinds of life-styles. In this particular case the son had to be taken from the home and temporary custody was awarded to the court, final custody to the father.

I wish this story had a happy ending but it doesn't. Mom refused any type of help. The only positive thing that came out of professional help was to get Dad and Jimmy away from Mom who was determined to vent her frustrations in a very violent manner. Jimmy had to go through a series of counseling sessions so that we could allay his fears and frustrations. We had to help him see that his situation was not a normal one.

Roger and Marion finally went their separate ways and divorced. Roger's leaving and subsequent divorce was really an act of love toward himself and his son. He was saying, in effect, that he didn't deserve to be treated that way, nor did his son. My guess is that Marion will continue to look for someone who needs to be used and abused and will probably someday find a person with those specific needs, and remarry.

Gerald, 44, was a millionaire. He owned property all over the country and flew to all parts of the globe. Gerald was a nationally known expert in his field. Although he had a beautiful, competent, and charming wife, he was a very angry man. He had a tremendously violent temper and a booming voice to go along with it. There were many times when his wife, Melody, was so shaken because of his outburst in public, that she left the room trembling in tears. She made contact with me due to the fact that she was so uptight and nervous around Gerald that she was beginning to develop gastro-intestinal problems and migraine headaches. That uptight feeling was consuming her energy and keeping her from being productive.

After surveying Gerald's and Melody's earlier childhood, I began to put the pieces together. When I asked Gerald to describe his earliest recollections of life, he couldn't go back beyond the age of 16, which was most unusual. At age 16, after hearing a gunshot, Gerald ran into the next room to see his father holding a gun to his head. His father had killed his mother and then proceeded to take his own life in front of Gerald. That same day his sister committed suicide. Gerald pulled down the steel curtain on his life and memory at that time. He was unable to go back and remember anything before that age, until he had therapy.

Gerald, in his mind had a right to be angry and bitter and

he developed a revengeful life-style.

As a young man striving to make it on his own, Gerald developed a tremendous amount of independence. He closed others out of his life. He would have to make it on his own because he was the lone survivor of his family. When he married Melody and they began to work together side by side in business, he would sometimes blow her away by his vicious explosion.

When asked what precipitated these explosions neither Melody nor Gerald was able to give an answer. All Gerald could say was that there was something inside him that would just snap and he would blow up. I asked Melody to write down sentences that they spoke to each other just before an explosion. We came to the conclusion that the key word which evoked a temper outburst was *why*. *Why* would send him skyward. He exploded because Melody was questioning his authority, his wisdom.

We were able to help Gerald and Melody in their marriage by simply eliminating the whys from Melody's vocabulary. We were able to cut down the outbursts by 75 percent in the first two weeks of therapy. In therapy, Gerald was given "permission" to talk about his feelings and his anger, and his need to show revenge.

As he began to open up, the relationship between Gerald and Melody began to become intimate. Even though Gerald had repelled everyone who tried to get close to him, he still had an urgent need to talk about his feelings, thoughts, fears, and anxieties. But since his tragic family background was not known to any of his acquaintances, and since everyone walked around him as if walking on eggshells, afraid of him, never getting to know him, Gerald had developed this hard protective shell around himself. He was so independent, so powerful, so all-knowing and competent that he didn't need others.

The marriage finally made it when we got Gerald and Melody to the point where they could sit and talk about anything. With lots of work and understanding on both their parts, we finally got the relationship on stable ground. Without logically looking at how we develop as adults, we could never have gotten Melody and Gerald to the place where they are today.

The important thing to remember about many life-styles is that they are founded on falsehood. We don't have to control or dominate or get others' attention in order to count for something.

As we view people, we can surmise that they will behave according to their life-style, to the way they have learned to view life selectively and with bias. It is important for us to be able to see that all of our experiences in early life are perceptions. Our feelings about our parents and siblings and our experiences come together to help us get a biased perception of ourselves. This biased, predictable behavior pattern is acted out in our life-style.

Action, Not Words

Why not try to get to know yourself and your mate better by doing each other's life-style? Play armchair psychologist for just a moment. Take turns asking each other the following questions:

1. How would you describe your mom or your dad? (Give seven or eight adjectives that would describe personality, make-up or temperament.)

2. How would you describe each of the siblings in your family?

3. How would you describe yourself as a kid, generally the elementary school-age child?

4. List 10 recollections about life, specifically early recollections. (These might be back as far as age two or three. Discuss these with each other.)

When each of you completes the exercise, review your answers. For question 1, the parent who had the most influence on you as a child is most likely to be the parent you described first. This is not to say that you got along best with that parent. In fact, that parent may have been absent from the home for most of your growing-up years, but that person, generally speaking, has been most influential in your life. We find that the person we describe first, in 95 percent of the cases, is the most influential person in our childhood. In describing your parents, if you use superlatives or adjectives preceded by "very," this is often an indication that you value that trait in your own life (very smart, very pretty, etc.).

In question 2, as you describe the siblings, begin to look for patterns, roles that are assumed by each of the children in your family. Diagram your family in similar fashion to what you did in the earlier chapter on birth order. Begin to make some intelligent guesses about how you see yourself, how your mate sees himself/herself, and get a feel for each other's life-style.

As you review question 3, generally speaking, the description you give yourself as a little kid is the exact description you would give yourself today as an adult. The little boy or girl you once were, you probably still are.

Question 4 might seem a bit too heavy for you to do, but

if you take the time to do it I think you'll find it to be enlightening. The very first recollection you had of life is symbolic of your entire life-style or the way you look at life. If it was a very negative kind of memory, that might mean that you tend to see things in a negative or pessimistic way. If all of your recollections were negative, I could make some assumptions regarding your negative outlook on life. If all the recollections were situations where you were the center of attention, people bringing you presents at Christmas and birthdays, we might say that your life-style could be centered around attention-getting. If some of your early recollections centered around breaking rules and regulations and being punished for them, we might make the guess that you are very controlling. You are good at keeping the rules and not very flexible.

You can make some intelligent deductions about yourself and your mate by looking at the pattern of early recollections.

Notes
1. See Ephesians 5:25.
2. See Matthew 6:2.

FIVE

One Plus One Equals One

Bobby asked his father, "Daddy, where did I come from?" His father, with a rather intense look on his face, began an eight-minute monologue telling his son "the facts of life." After the discourse the four-and-a-half year old looked up with an inquisitive expression on his face and said, "Daddy, I mean where did *I* come from? Billy came from Albany, New York."

I couldn't write a book about marital relationship without spending some time talking about communication. Even though "communication" is an overused word today, good communication is still one of the most important single factors in a marriage. If your marriage is a typical one I think it's safe to say that you spend fewer than five minutes a day in real communication.

As a psychologist I find that men and women are basically afraid to communicate, to tell each other who they are, to express their innermost thoughts, needs and feelings. For our purpose, let's assume that when I use the word *communication* I mean "a sharing of yourself verbally and nonverbally in such a way as to enable someone else to understand what you've said and how you feel." Communication involves not only the sharing of words, but, just as importantly, the skills of listening and understanding.

Recently, a full-page ad in the *Wall Street Journal* caught my eye. Sperry Rand Corporation devoted an entire page (which had to cost a bundle) to the art of listening, telling the readers that all their employees—from secretaries to corporate executives—go through listening seminars. When big business learns that it pays to listen, we ought to take note. Because the bottom line for business, I am sure, is the increased productivity as a result of good listening habits. If it's good enough for Sperry Rand it should be good enough for our own marriages. Simply listening to our mates is taking a giant step toward becoming one in marriage.

Communication between husband and wife usually goes something like this. Husband walks in the door at night and greets wife, "Hello! I'm home. How was your day?"

"OK," wife responds.

"What's for dinner?"

"Chicken."

Now, what was really said in this conversation? "I don't want to talk about my day. I don't want to share my feelings. What I am concerned about is what's for dinner."

Generally, the amount and quality of communication between a married couple reveals a lot about their marriage. For example, have you ever been curious about your neighbor's sexual relationship? Go ahead, admit it! All you need to do is ask your neighbor, "Harriet, how would you describe your communication with John?" Whatever the answer is, it is probably a description of what their sexual relationship is really like. As a counselor I have seen many good marriages wither, starve, or go under due to non-nourishment, and communication between couples is essential nourishment.

We Don't Know How

Why do we not communicate with each other? I believe there are various reasons; I will discuss four of them here. Perhaps the most prevalent one is that we haven't learned the skill of communication. The husband who walks in the door with "Hi, honey! I'm home. What's for dinner? Where's the mail?" is showing that he isn't skilled at meaningful communication, nor does he really care. Most of the time these verbal responses communicate that "I as your husband (or wife) really am not interested in carrying on any type of feedback. Nor am I interested in expressing how *I* feel." Naturally, if we are really disinterested in our mate's feelings we aren't going to do much to learn to communicate with him or her.

Jack, 43, and Dottie, 41, had been married for 21 years and were raising five children. Being a blue-collar family, they had to scrape for every nickel they could get; but basically things went well throughout most of their apparently typical marriage. However, when I first saw Dottie she had just been released from a residential psychiatric treatment center. She had suffered, in her words, "a nervous breakdown." Dottie told me that she had been a good mother and wife. She had always been the kind of person she thought others wanted her to be. She was always doing things for other people. She was sacrificially going without things in her own life. When I asked if she and Jack ever got away together for a weekend, leaving the children home, she proudly answered that they *never* left the children.

As Dottie related her situation to me I had the hunch that their sex life wasn't very good. I guessed right. It was down-right terrible! In 21 years of marriage Dottie had never experienced an orgasm, or any physical satisfaction sexually with her husband.

As I pressed Dottie for some background information as to what precipitated the breakdown she told me that the washing machine had a breakdown first, about six weeks prior to hers. Jack assured her that he would fix it this weekend . . . then the next weekend. . . . That time never came and things began to close in on Dottie. You can imagine how important a washing machine is to a family with five children! When Jack continued to put off fixing the washing machine Dottie essentially chose to "go under." Notice I said *chose?* Mental illness is not "caught" but is learned behavior which *serves a purpose in one's life* either consciously or subconsciously. In this case, Dottie's choosing to go under was her way of making her husband pay attention to her. She decided to cop out of life for a three-week stay—which by the way cost her husband $5,500! It seems he would have been money ahead to call the Maytag repairman!

There was still another factor involved. Jack, although he couldn't find time or money to fix some of the appliances around the home, found money enough to buy a second-hand pick-up truck. That incident contributed toward the final blow to Dottie.

Jack finally woke up to the fact that he had been negligent as a husband. Dottie's absence from the home made him experience what a tremendous contribution she made to the entire family. He had to take off work and become a homemaker for about a three-week period. (You can bet the washing machine got fixed!)

The real Jack surfaced when he began to demonstrate to Dottie, both before and after her release from the treatment center, how much he really cared for her. Not only did he show more consideration of her needs and feelings by helping with the domestic chores, he also contracted with me—but more importantly with himself—that each day he was going to make special time so that he and his wife could have some quiet moments of sharing with each other.

As soon as Dottie came home from the residential treatment center he began to take her for walks (without the children) where they strolled arm in arm for a couple of miles. They shared their thoughts and feelings, deepening their relationship. This experience was like a refreshing breeze to a stale marriage that very much needed to be rekindled. My response when Dottie had told me they *never* left the children was to say, "How sad that you couldn't think enough of yourself and your relationship with Jack to take off for a weekend now and then." She had said they couldn't afford it. However, in most homes we enjoy color TV, fairly nice furniture and basically the finer things in life. We don't hesitate to put a washer, dryer or TV set on a revolving charge account, but we can't come up with a couple hundred dollars for a very special weekend away. We have a difficult time investing in our relationship.

Dottie shared with Jack that she thought she had done her very best, on several occasions, to communicate that she was hurting. She thought she was telling him she needed his help, but he was oblivious to her needs and selfish in thinking only of himself. Jack's and Dottie's communication was superficial, a malady in most marriages today. It took action and commitment on both their parts to begin to turn their marriage around.

During an individual session with Dottie I planted a seed in her mind that maybe she could become *involved* in her sex life with Jack rather than just being a *recipient*. Dottie agreed to at least experiment. (Keep in mind that Dottie and Jack were blue-collar workers with limited income. For them an evening out to a cafeteria for dinner might only happen once every six months.)

I suggested that Dottie take her husband out to dinner at a swanky local hotel. Her first concern was for the financial consideration. I successfully convinced her that instead of a $5,500 stay in a psychiatric residential treatment center, she would be money ahead by investing in the relationship. She decided to become a part of the therapy in a very action-oriented manner.

Dottie made reservations for dinner and a hotel room and even placed fresh flowers in the room. After a very enjoyable dinner together she asked if Jack would like to go for a walk. As they walked along the lagoon-like area, Dottie steered him past the reserved room with key in hand. Suddenly she plunged the key into the keyhole, turned the knob and in the same motion yanked Jack into the room. Yes, this was going to be *the* night.

Dottie told me that she had written a love note in lipstick on the mirror—this was the lady who couldn't adequately communicate her feelings before. I never did find out what the note said but when I saw Jack a couple of days later, his first remarks were, "Doc, I don't know what you did, but whatever you did it was beautiful."

Jack initially failed to see that I didn't do much of anything. Dottie's action was encouraged by his demonstrating his love, concern and affection for her that made her *feel* like trying once again! Dottie experienced her first orgasm in 21 years of marriage that evening in the hotel.

Jack took the pledge that Dottie was worth loving and worth a full sexual relationship. They made it! They turned it around! Dottie and Jack now have a relationship that exemplifies "One Plus One Equals One," not only physically, but also emotionally. They made each other's feelings a priority in their lives. Now, nothing comes before God and each other in their family.

I couldn't help but think of them as frolicking teenagers when I saw them in the office the next time. They couldn't keep their hands off each other. It was great to see this rekindled love in two people who really did love each other but needed to learn to communicate to each other, to confront self and each other.

We Are Afraid

A second reason for not communicating in marriage, besides never learning to do so, is that many husbands and wives admit to being afraid of sharing their real selves with their mates. They are afraid that if they told their mates how they really felt about certain issues their mates would somehow reject them.

Action, Not Words

On a sheet of paper, draw a horizontal line about an inch from the top and a vertical line down the middle. In the left-hand column, above the horizontal line, write the words "real self," and on the right-hand side write the words "ideal self." Now take a couple of minutes to write down a description of your "real self," the self *you* know you really are. Now devote a couple of minutes describing the "ideal self," the self you would like everyone else to see you as. Now, what self does your mate know? Does your mate know the real self? If he/she doesn't know the real self, you are one of the many thousands of people who is afraid to open up and share because you fear rejection. Think how special it would be to have your mate know and love the real you without any qualifications whatsoever.

We carry this fear of sharing our real selves even into our relationship with God. We put limits on Almighty God! Some of us act in such a way as to communicate that God wouldn't be able to forgive us if He knew that we did this or that. In essence, when we do that we are really limiting God and putting Him in His place. If God is the God He says He is, our Creator, He is certainly big enough to know how we're made and to forgive us of our transgressions. But instead of confessing to God, "letting our hair down" before Him, we try to hide our feelings, fears, needs, frustrations and apprehensions for fear He won't love us anymore because we are weak. How foolish! He wants us to be totally unique. Perhaps the weakness you think you have is just a special characteristic that makes you you.

Take a look back at your real and ideal self you described earlier. Which self do you communicate to God? Do you try to conceal your real self? You see, if God knows everything about you, even the number of hairs on your head, He certainly knows your real heart, motives and missions in life.

I think many of us share only our "ideal self" with God just as we try to share only our ideal self with our mates. If we are going to communicate openly and honestly with God in prayer, we must first be open and honest with ourselves and with others. If a couple can't be open and honest with each other, I doubt that they can share with their heavenly Father. Keep in mind that Jesus can save us only when we acknowledge that we are imperfect. If we were perfect we wouldn't have any need for Him. It's when we call to Him from the depths of our heart that we are truly touched and feel His closeness. Then He can forgive us and accept us into full fellowship with Him.

As God forgives you when you open up to Him, so must you forgive once your mate shares deep feelings with you, or else your marriage will not flourish.

Too Much Trouble

Another reason for failure to communicate is that it is essentially too much trouble for many couples. It's much easier to avoid, suppress and repress our thoughts and feelings. This reason is closely tied to the fact that many of us don't communicate because our self-worth or self-esteem is so low that it really doesn't make much difference if we share opinions because our opinions aren't worth expressing. Often our opinions are shot down by people we care about. If this happens frequently enough we become gun-shy and draw ourselves further into our protective shell. If we don't communicate our true feelings then we can't be rejected or hurt.

This kind of hurt is buried within us and causes many kinds of emotional and psychological problems. Very few people are able to continue to tuck away hurts without having those hurts surface in some ugly ways within their lives.

Think of your emotional self as a teakettle on a stove with the steam being your emotions and feelings. If you don't have the opportunity to let out your emotions and feelings in a constant and free-flowing manner, then sooner or later you get to the point where you blow your top! Then the anger and the hurt that is directed toward another person is usually a very destructive kind of communication. Lack of self-worth in either mate leads to indifference, and indifference leads to not caring. This in turn often leads to divorce.

Lucy was divorced for the first time at age 19, the second time at 23 and the third time at 28. Lucy's first husband was a rather shiftless, unfaithful, irresponsible young man. He had joined the navy and left her home—high, dry, and pregnant.

Only four months after being divorced from her first husband, Lucy married Al. On the surface Al looked like he was everything a husband should be. It turned out that he had a problem with drugs and eventually lost his job; he was also unfaithful to his wife. Again Lucy filed for dissolution of their marriage. With much determination Lucy vowed that she was through with men and that she would never marry again. But then she found Rowdy Raymond who not only had the skills of her first two husbands but was a wife beater as well.

How is it that Lucy could find three such losers in such a short period of time? To really answer this question sufficiently, I did a life-style analysis on her. I took the time to have her describe herself, her parents, her siblings and her early recollections of her childhood. Then we went step by step through every relationship she had ever had with men in her life.

It was in all these descriptions and recollections of life that we found the reasons for Lucy behaving the way she did. My assumption was that she sought out people who reinforced her life-style—which was that she was not worth loving. I figured that her father was either absent from the home or was very much a controller. I assumed that he was good at withdrawing affection from his daughter, Lucy. How right I was! Lucy's mom was the dominant figure in the family. She made most of the decisions. Her husband was a businessman who was wrapped up in his business. He was good at keeping people, particularly those close to him, at arm's-length. Lucy said she never saw her dad cry, he never held her, he wasn't a good masculine image to have in the home with a daughter.

Lucy had an older brother and an older sister. Her older sister was little Miss Perfect who did almost everything right. She was a top student, an achiever and Mom's good helper. Her older brother was the athlete and the president of his high school senior class and hoped to join his dad in business in later life.

Through the life-style analysis Lucy saw that there really were some logical reasons for her to behave as she did. She was the one who was truant from school, gave people a bad time, and was essentially everything a young woman shouldn't be—according to her mother. She was promiscuous as early as 13, had an abortion at 16 and married at 19. If she couldn't be the best, she chose to become the worst. She drove her parents up the wall with her abhorrent behavior.

One session I challenged Lucy with the fact that she selected people to marry who were no good for her, who would mistreat her and behave in a very unloving manner. She asked me, "Dr. Leman, why would anyone marry someone they knew would mistreat them?" I answered that people marry people like that because their basic self-worth is so lacking. All of her marriages reflected her self-image—she wasn't worth loving and any decent, faithful man wouldn't care for her. Her husbands all reinforced her basic life theme, which was that she really wasn't worth loving.

In all of her sexual experiences with young men Lucy admitted to never having had any real sexual satisfaction. She admitted to feeling used, cheap and frustrated. She never expected her husbands to be supportive, loving and caring. She never saw a male in her home who was capable of showing such tender feelings. Lucy's life brings to the forefront the need for us, as men, to be loving, kind and gentle to our daughters. To have a close, loving and warm relationship is important because we are representing what men are all about.

Lucy's first recollection of life was sitting, looking out of a window, watching little children playing on the edge of a pond, skipping rocks across the water. She was thinking to herself that she wished she was out with the children having fun. That recollection is symbolic in that she never entered into the mainstream of life. She was always at the periphery, looking on. She had such a fear of rejection that she set her sights very low, took whatever came to her and, in the process, was raked over the coals by many men in her life.

Lucy learned through the life-style analysis that it was very important for her to get the attention of men (any man) since she didn't have the attention of her father. It didn't make any difference if the attention was negative or positive as long as it was attention. I wish I could say there is a happy ending to Lucy's life at this juncture, but there isn't. She's just beginning to put the pieces together, to become at least open to the possibility of dating once again.

We're presently working on her thinking of herself as a worthwhile human being. In the dating process, we're trying to reinforce that she isn't to be *used* by anybody, for anything, for any reason. Because of the insight provided by her life-style analysis, she made the commitment to relearn some things that had been ingrained in her life. Lucy is going to make it. She's going to begin to treat herself as a positive, loving person. The life-style she held about herself, the opinion of herself, was in fact a big lie. She felt that she only counted in life when she was noticed.

No Success

The fourth reason why couples don't communicate is that they never had any success at it. Every time they tried to open up and share their feelings they were shot down. They were tuned out. Their candle was blown out. Being tuned out can start in life as early as childhood. Do you remember running to Mom and Dad with some exciting discovery only to be met with a disinterested, "Uh-huh"? The message is clear—"What you have to say is not worth my time or attention." When we learn at so young an age to put a protective shield over our feelings, it is very difficult to truly share with our loved ones later on in life. I see people daily who are turtlelike, who have on previous occasions stuck their heads out only to have them chopped off. They've gone near the hot stove one too many times and gotten burned and they've concluded that they are going to protect themselves from ever entering into life's arena.

In order to communicate with someone else, we really must be able to be in communication with our own feelings and thoughts. For us to be secure enough to take the time to listen we need to have that self-worth and that security within ourselves as a prime prerequisite.

Communication really is a very complex entity. Most of us have never had the opportunity to communicate with anyone. It's a sad commentary on the relationships we have with our mates, relatives, children and friends. We spend too much time on frilly, surface communication which adds no depth to any relationship.

There are basically two reasons why we have no success at good communication: (1) we don't listen, (2) we don't perceive what is being said.

Listening is at least a third of the communication process, the other thirds being the sharing of self and the understanding that follows the listening. When your mate is talking to you and you are thinking about what you're going to say in response, then you're not listening. You are really not communicating because you're too busy figuring out how you are going to defend yourself. The bantering of words back and forth is probably going to escalate to such a point that there is no further talking whatsoever. We really don't get close to the point of good communication if we are too busy thinking of our counterattack while our mate is talking. This condition is another symptom of a competitive marriage and, like most things in life that are competitive, if somebody wins, somebody loses. Who's winning your marriage? We will be talking more about competition in marriage. Competition destroys the formula "One Plus One Equals One."

Action, Not Words

One way you can start to increase communication in your marriage is to do the following exercise. Find a time when you can simply sit back and listen to your mate. Don't interrupt and don't think about what you are going to say. Just simply listen. Then communicate verbally and nonverbally that you really understand what your mate is trying to say. Reinforce that you are interested and that you care enough to listen in depth.

Even if you are listening you may not be *perceiving* what your mate is saying. There may be a difference between what you want to say, and what you've actually said or what your mate hears and what your mate thinks he or she hears. It really can become very complicated.

Action, Not Words

An exercise I frequently give to couples who come for marital help is to sit facing each other. Then choose a subject. One person will begin telling the other person how he/she really feels on the matter without being interrupted. The other person then has the task of telling the speaker what he or she has just said. The first speaker either affirms, denies, or modifies what he or she meant and what the mate heard.

Then the role is reversed. A little practice in this type of communication will soon make you aware of how you misconstrue what your mate is trying to say, how you read into statements things that were not meant to be.

Five Levels of Communication

In one of the best books I've ever read about communication, *Why Am I Afraid to Tell You Who I Am?* by John Powell, he talks about the five levels of communication.[1] I'll mention them just briefly to give you an idea of the leveling effect of communication and the need for us to strive to get as deep a level of communication as possible within our marriage.

The fifth level—cliche´ conversation. The following little catch phrases are examples of cliche´ conversation: "Hey, how have you been?" "Good to see you." "How's the family?" "Say, you're sure looking good" (we usually reserve this one for older people who really don't look very well). Just for the fun of it, try something interesting. The next time someone acknowledges you at work with, "Hi! How are you?" Stop. Make a U-turn, walk alongside of him and begin to tell him how you *really* are. The other person may turn different shades of the rainbow, but you will be taking a step in the right direction!

The fourth level—reporting fact about others. Ah! This is easy! These are words and conversations that are designed to keep us aloof and removed from people. We talk about others but we avoid getting ourselves in the middle of the conversation in any kind of emotional matter.

The third level—ideas and judgments. Here we begin to approach an area of real communication. We are finally beginning to tell someone about our ideas, thoughts and judgments. We still tend to be somewhat apprehensive and if we meet with disapproval we sometimes will modify our thoughts and judgments more to the other person's liking. We appear to back off and take a more palatable stance on an issue or one that might be designed to seek the approval of the other person. Here we tend to jump out of the way of criticism at all cost.

The second level—feelings and emotions. Now as husband and wife, we begin to share the feelings that are underneath the ideas and judgments expressed. A common example might be when the husband gets up and leaves the dinner table every night and never says anything about the meal or how much effort his wife exerted to prepare it; he leaves her feeling like she is his maid or servant. Wives are not for using in any sense of the word. Wouldn't it be nice if husbands could say, "I really feel special because you took the time and effort to make such a lovely meal"; or, how about just before the meal is served the husband asks his wife to be seated and proceeds to serve her first, in front of the children? Chances are she would have to be revived from her position on the floor. Here's an opportunity to demonstrate to your children that the priority in your life is your marriage and each other's feelings. Children need to see husbands meeting the needs of their wives in a practical, direct, straightforward manner. We are the models of marriage that our children are going to go out into the world with. They are going to go into life drawing conclusions of what life is all about from their experience in the home watching the relationship between their mom and their dad.

The first level—complete emotional and personal truth-

fulness in communication. For us to survive in marriage this is a must. We must develop an openness and honesty within our relationship that says, "I can tell you how I really feel without you judging that feeling." This level of communication is very difficult because of the possibility of our being rejected.

I'm not much for bumper stickers, particularly the ones many Christians put on their cars such as, "Caution, in case of rapture this vehicle will be unmanned." Wonderful! But there is one bumper sticker that really catches my eye. It reads, "Christians aren't perfect, they're just forgiven." If we as husbands and wives would dedicate ourselves to the principle that we aren't perfect and that we don't expect our mates to be perfect we would initially heighten the probability of real communication within marriage. There's no way we can make our mates, our children, or anyone else, be perfect.

How often have we asked God to please change someone else, change the selfishness, the drinking problem, the bad habits? I need to ask God to change *me*. I can't change someone else's drinking problem but He can, in His time and wisdom. It's only through asking God to change myself that I start to understand others.

Action, Not Words

If you are looking for a unique way to communicate with each other, you might consider doing what one couple did. They made the commitment to pray aloud in bed each night, in each other's arms. This activity enabled them to turn the corner in their marriage; they began to open up and share their thoughts and feelings. A special warmth and closeness of being in each other's arms and holding each other followed. Their stresses, problems, fears and worries were taken to God in prayer, together. Not only did their communication with each other improve, but their communication and openness with God became a mighty, working force in both their lives. In this case one plus one plus One equals one!

Don't knock it until you've tried it! And besides, there might even be some positive aftereffects of holding each other close.

Communication is a very difficult concept for us to master. Most of us stay at a superficial level. And yet, if I don't make an attempt to deal with the important things in life and in marriage on a strong, intimate communicative basis, then my mate is not going to enter into a risk-like situation and share herself openly with me. We will never be one.

Right alongside this problem of communication lies another—the inability to express our emotions in an acceptable, satisfying way. Read on . . .

Note
1. John Powell, *Why Am I Afraid to Tell You Who I Am?* (Niles, IL: Argus Communications, 1969).

SIX

Nothing More Than Feelings

Before we will ever become one in marriage we must be brave enough to share with each other our real self, our feelings that are unique to each individual. One way to know how our mate feels is to spend time walking in his or her shoes. It's a little like the time Tarzan came in from a long arduous day, snapped at Jane and said, "But, Jane, you don't understand . . . ! It's a *jungle* out there!"

Since we can never completely walk in our mate's shoes, or crawl inside his or her skin, we will have to let our mate into our private world, into the arena of our emotions.

Most of us have learned *not* to share feelings. In fact, we all can probably recall experiences in our lives when we did reveal our real feelings and somebody was there to extinguish them almost immediately. We don't have to be very old before we begin to smother those wonderful emotions God gave us. Yes, we're born with emotions. A little child expresses his emotions—joy, anger, sadness, fear, love—openly and honestly until his parents or others scold, threaten or beat them out of him—or push them deep inside him.

When my own son, Kevey, was two and a half we had a couple over for dinner. Kevey turned to my wife and said, "Mommy, what's her name?"

My wife turned adoringly toward our son and answered, "That's Mrs. McVay."

Kevey said, "Oh . . . I hate her!" (A new word he evidently picked up that day.) Children are so wonderfully straightforward. They'll tell you exactly how they feel. It's only with negative experiences in sharing our feelings that we develop into the phonies many of us are.

Probably the emotion we have the most trouble dealing with on a day-to-day basis is anger. I'm not going to talk about anger in this chapter because it's important enough to devote a separate chapter to.

In this chapter I want you to learn five things about feelings: (1) your feelings aren't "right" or "wrong"; (2) you have a right to express your feelings; (3) you don't always have to act on your feelings; (4) you should never ask your mate, "Why do you feel that way?" (because the emphasis is then placed on the cause and not on the feeling); and (5) feelings draw you closer to your mate, but judgments push you apart.

Your Feelings Aren't "Right" or "Wrong"

For us to understand our own feelings and our mate's feelings, we must come to the resolution that *feelings aren't right or wrong,* they are just your own feelings. Negative or positive feelings do not make us good or bad people. We are good people. God created us "in his own image," and said "it was very good."[1]

If everything about us, as God created us, is good, why then are we reluctant to share our feelings?

As I mentioned earlier, sometimes the natural inclination to show our feelings is beaten out of us very early in life. We are taught to *not* be rude, to *not* hurt people, to *not* get too excited, to *not* express too much affection, to *not* grieve, to *not* cry. As we grow more "mature" we may choose to intellectualize and rationalize why we can't or don't share our feelings: we don't want to rock the boat; we want the waters of life to be smooth; it's easier to be a plastic person than a warm, caring one. Since we are not used to sharing our emotions or seeing other persons share theirs there is a danger that we might be misunderstood.

Let me give you an example. If I make this statement, "I think you're very beautiful," you might react with one of these thoughts: "I feel inferior to you"; "I feel ugly"; "I feel threatened by you"; "I feel sexually aroused"; "I feel like I'd like to hit you." If I know that my comment would trigger any one of these reactions within you, I might rationalize, "I'd better not express how I feel about her or else I might threaten or hurt her or rock the boat." When the person you are reacting to in this way is your wife or your husband then you are leaving your marriage wide open to destruction.

What happens when we repress our natural emotions, our feelings? Most of us pay for this repression in many ways. Many of the people I see in my private practice who suffer from such things as ulcers, gastro-intestinal disorders, headaches, migraines, cluster headaches, backaches, back spasms, muscle spasms, cramps in their legs and feet, are usually people who have chosen to repress their feelings. These emotions have then expressed themselves physiologically throughout the person's body in one form or another. It is important for us to realize that we do not have to repress our emotions. They are what we feel. We have no reason to apologize for how we feel. However, often we may have to apologize for what we *do*.

If we act out in a hostile or negative way, then we must be held accountable for that action. When you strike out you may feel angry but you have no right to hurt someone physically, or cause someone else to smother his emotions, because of your negative feelings.

You Have a Right to Express Your Feelings

Since your emotions are neither "right" nor "wrong," you have a right to express your feelings. But what happens when you want to sit down and share but you meet the great wall of resistance? I think of Betty Jane, 24, who had tried on numerous occasions to express her feelings of neglect, worry, frustration, fear and anger about her non-relationship with her husband. Every time she began to express her feelings he would, in bull-like fashion, simply run over her. He would cut her off, intimidate her and tell her to get off his case.

Finally, at my urging, Betty Jane wrote her husband a personal love letter and sent it to his place of business. She had the opportunity to write out how she felt, to express her emotions. This letter began to help make some inroads toward getting Betty Jane and Wayne to communicate with each other. Wayne's life-style seemed to say that he counted only when he was in control, dominating and intimidating. He was secure only when he was the winner. Any time Betty Jane would mount an offensive toward him he would simply shore up his defense and turn into a verbal steamroller, running all over his wife. The letter, in this case, was a very simple tool that was used effectively to get Betty Jane and Wayne to at least start discussing their feelings with each other. Often a letter can reveal our emotions when discussing them would only start an argument.

Try to be very sensitive when your mate, or someone else, is opening up his very innermost feelings. A lot of us can't handle the discomfort we experience when we're dealing with true human emotion. I know people who cannot handle others sharing their grief. We impose on them our time clock of how long they are entitled to be grieving over the loss of a loved one. Remarks such as "it's time to get on with your life" tell them that you really don't want to hear about it anymore. The feelings of grief come to us at such a gut level that we want to candy-coat them so they are palatable. If a person is not allowed to fully express grief, he or she may never "get over" it.

Instead of continually turning him off because you can't handle that sensitive area, why not try grieving with the person? Offer a word of sympathy or cry with him. Bring your caring feelings out in the open. It's a sad commentary when we're afraid to reach out and touch people. It's pathetic when someone reaches out to us and we respond with a denial of feelings, both theirs and our own.

If you have been denying your feelings over a long period of time you may have to drag them out and begin to exercise them. If your feelings are to be worthwhile and productive they must be kept warm and alive. It reminds me of a story about the two old men who were ice fishing on a lake in New York state. After fishing all day and catching nothing they were turning their thoughts toward picking up and going home. A 14-year-old boy came along and proceeded to cut a hole in the ice within a hundred feet of them. Almost immediately he began to catch one fish after another. One of the amazed men yelled across to the boy, "Hey, I don't understand it! We've been fishing all day and haven't caught anything. What's your secret? What are you using for bait?" The 14-year-old muttered something unintelligible. With the older man's insistence the boy finally spit a wad of worms into his hand and said, "You gotta keep your worms warm!" In our case, feelings are like worms: you have to keep them warm! You can't let them get chilly or stale or they will stop being productive.

How do you begin to share your own feelings, so you can understand the feelings of those around you? One way is to be willing to take the time to sit and talk with each other. God didn't give us "see-through" foreheads. We cannot read each other's minds, though we often insist we can. There are times when you have to tell, and there are times when you have to ask. Begin today to share your feelings. Be especially sensitive to and encourage your children's and your mate's expressions of emotions.

You Don't Always Have to Act on Your Feelings

Although God has created us to experience the full gamut of feelings, it is important to realize that we can choose not to act on our feelings. This would be a terrible world if we all went around acting out our feelings. In psychological terms we refer to the libidinous forces that are running around our body as the "Id." The id is the portion of the personality that drives us to act on impulse.

Just imagine what would happen if we all acted on impulse. For example, what do you do when you are in a restaurant and all of a sudden feelings of sexual arousal come over you? I realize that you really could act on your emotions right then, but you'd sure never go back to that restaurant again, would you? And I'm sure your mate would never want to go out to dinner with you again.

Many years ago I knew a young man who was so fiercely competitive on the baseball field that he threw temper tantrums. As a man in his early twenties he was ejected from many ball games for throwing his bat, kicking the dirt, stomping his feet and cussing out umpires. He was overdriven with the desire to be terribly competitive. He felt he *had* to win. He allowed his feelings to get the best of him. Not only did they surface but they dominated him during the entire ball game. It got to the point where his teammates tiptoed around him and avoided him altogether.

Acting out feelings in this way is often a controlling type of behavior. Many times when we allow our feelings to rise to the top we do it for a purpose. We often get our own way through being powerful, explosive or—going in the other direction—by choosing to withdraw, being sheepish or moody. An example of the "quiet-type" controller is the "depressed" wife who complains all the time about not getting enough attention. What she is really doing is exercising a neurotic type of attention-getting—it's her way of keeping her mate knuckled under to get more attention from him. Most people who come to me with *depression* are showing purposive behavior. Such a one might be displaying his feelings of depression to punish himself, or his or her mate.

Many times people who act out their feelings in an

unrestrained way choose to cop-out by saying, "I'm sorry, but that's just the way I am." That's putting up an invisible shield around himself. It's a way of saying, "I refuse to change. I'm going to dominate and control by not becoming part of it." How sad!

If you feel angry, like punching someone or spitting on them or something equally antisocial, you don't *have* to act on your emotions. What's important is that you realize how you feel and that you express those feelings in an acceptable manner. Now, suppose that in a restaurant a waitress is discourteous. You may feel very put out and you may have to weigh the possibility of expressing this anger to the waitress or to the manager. There might be times when it would be best not to express the feeling verbally, for example if there are several people dining with you. But you still have the right to express how you feel by not leaving her a tip. However, such is not the case in your marital relationship. It is usually best to express the feeling—again in a non-violent, socially acceptable way—rather than tucking it away. By expressing those feelings we become more solidly bonded than just "two ships that pass in the night."

Paul told the Ephesians to "not let the sun go down while you are still angry."[2] In other words, don't go to bed with unexpressed feelings toward your mate. Let him know the feelings you are experiencing, even if you don't choose to act on them.

A Question You Never Ask

One question you should *never* ask your mate is, "Why do you feel that way?"

First of all, asking why your mate feels the way he does

provides the groundwork for immediate resistance and defensiveness. The word "why" can be a stopper, one that ends communication instantaneously. Remember, if you really want to know how your mate feels you must be willing to devote time to honest dialogue. A "why" question is an intrusion into your mate's thoughts and feelings and can prohibit you from hearing feelings of a deeper origin.

As a couple you must each work toward acceptance when your mate is sharing: concentrate on what is being said, listen for the feelings, watch the face and body language, absorb as much as you are able. Asking why takes you away from an accepting environment into a judgmental atmosphere. In order to judge someone you have to be superior. Right? It's the traditional superior/inferior relationships that have gotten us into great difficulty in our contemporary marriages.

What your mate is telling you might be very different from what you want to hear. It's important to keep in mind that you don't have to agree to everything your husband or wife says. That would soon lead to a very dull relationship. But, out of respect and love, you should listen to each other, value each other's opinions and work out a solution, if one is needed, that is mutually satisfying. It comes back to the need each of us has to know that our mate cares about us.

I'm sure there are thousands of married couples who have tried to share their "real self" with their mates, but felt intimidated by one little three letter word, "why" or its variation, "how come?" John and Marcy were one such couple. Marcy, a retiring sort, finally got up enough nerve to talk with John about her feelings concerning his secretary whom he raved about constantly. After three short sentences John retorted with, "Why do you feel that way?" Marcy, in tears, immediately hightailed it for her bedroom.

How very different that scene could have been if only he had patiently and lovingly listened to her. The "why" to Marcy implied that she had no right to feel the way she obviously felt. Remember, we each have a right to our feelings; our feelings are neither right nor wrong, they are just our feelings and should never be judged! *Why* should we selectively eliminate *why* from our vocabulary when we are discussing feelings with loved ones? (1) It inhibits communication; (2) it implies the need to defend our feelings; (3) it inhibits acceptance; and (4) many times it triggers defensiveness.

A little three-year-old runs to his mom and says, "Mommy, Mommy, look at this picture I painted for you!"

If Mommy replies with "*Why* did you paint a picture for me?" that takes the wonderful focus of gift-giving away and tells the child that Mom needs to know more elaborate reasons why the child cares for her. The child may be too young to vocalize his deeper feelings but old enough to believe that his art work, which he so diligently worked on, is enough to convey his very special, loving feelings toward his mother.

So remember! Refrain from asking "why" unless you want to keep that emotional distance between you and your mate. If you don't want to take the time to talk, "why" will end the discussion quite rapidly!

Feelings Draw You Closer, Judgments Push You Apart

One of the reasons we have difficulty understanding our

own and our mate's feelings is that we layer the feelings with judgments, opinions, values and sheer surface-level type of communication. When we do try to get close to expressing feelings, we tend to blame those feelings on other people. "You made me really mad." "She makes me so angry, I could scream!" Or even, "You made me love you." Statements such as these are examples of how we project another person as the source of our anger or other emotion. The fact is, *our feelings are made, manufactured and distributed by our own self!* Anger, joy, happiness, fear—every emotion comes from within us. No one else can make us angry. No one else can make us happy. These emotions grow from our own depths.

Try to begin expressing yourself with "I" statements rather than "you" statements. Instead of saying, "You make me so angry!" say, "I feel very angry when you say things like that." H. Norman Wright, in his book, *The Pillars of Marriage,* says that "there are four main ways to describe feelings verbally: (1) Identify or name the feeling. 'I feel angry'; 'I feel sad'; 'I feel good about you.' (2) Use similes and metaphors. . . . 'I feel squelched'; 'I felt like a cool breeze going through the air.' (3) Report the type of action your feelings urge you to do. 'I feel like hugging you'; 'I wish I could hit you.' (4) Use figures of speech, such as, 'The sun is smiling on me today'; 'I feel like a dark cloud is following me around today.'"[3]

Learning to express your feelings, recognizing that nobody but your own self is responsible for your feelings, will help you to stop being judgmental. It is important to make a commitment to not offend each other by being judgmental. It is important that you accept each other as you really are.

Think how fulfilling it would be if you could tell your mate your frustrations, your deep love and hidden concerns and know that your mate would not judge or condemn those feelings. You might soften the sharing of your feelings by saying, "I'm not sure why I'm feeling this, but right now I'm feeling hurt, I'm feeling angry, I feel revengeful, I feel left out." Whatever that feeling might be, try to express it.

One way to discover if you are judging the *person* rather than the *act* is to see if you include "that" in your statement. If you preface your feeling with the word "that" then it is a *judgment* and not a *feeling*: "I feel *that* you are always finding fault with me." That's an opinion or judgment, not a feeling. In order for your emotion communication to be effective you must not put the other person on the defensive, which is exactly what the little word "that" does. Instead try, "I feel very hurt inside when golf is more important every Sunday than I am."

A very serious problem in being judgmental of a person is that we tend to harbor our judgments, bringing them up long after the fact. I call this activity "bone-digging." Long after the situation is over, after the dust has settled, if true emotions and feelings have never been expressed, the "bone-digger" digs up those bones of long-gone emotions. Such an exercise is rarely productive. Only during therapy does it pay to be a bone-digger. If there is a need to go back and examine a relationship, if there are some old bones back there that are still causing problems today, then it is imperative that we dig them up, examine them, talk about our feelings, then bury them once and for all. "Old bones" are often deep hurts or imagined injustices that we have tried to bury but which resurface to hinder the growth of a successful relationship.

If your marital relationship is not based upon openness and honesty, then chances are your relationship will be adolescent-like, where all the manifestations of adolescence—jealousy, accusations, bantering back and forth, pouting, getting mad, leaving in a huff, running to your room or home to mother—are evident. Those kinds of behaviors will be found in relationships that are stagnant, non-growing.

As a psychologist, I always take time to tell my clients about myself. I tell them that I am married, that I have a lovely wife and three children, that I enjoy family therapy and private practice, that I'm action-oriented and that my true mission in life is to "get rid of my clients." I see that getting rid of them is an encouraging process which says that they don't have to be dependent on me to make progress.

I begin to share with them my unique self. I usually mention that "I graduated very near the bottom of my high school class and couldn't get admitted to college—I applied to over 100 of them unsuccessfully. (I eventually got into one; sorry, I can't give you the name—we have a working agreement . . .)" I share with my clients, and in seminars where I am teaching, some of the inadequacies I feel as a person, some of the fears I have, some of my priorities in life—which are primarily my marriage and my children and my reliance upon God for spiritual strength and direction. I begin to open up to them. I tell them that contrary to what I was taught in graduate school, I'll be brave enough to tell them how I feel. I begin to share with them real experiences in my life that I think might be helpful for them to hear.

I don't share my deepest feelings with them on our first meeting. I plant a seed that it's OK for us to communicate about anything we want to talk about. I am going to become a part of that process. I'm not going to be some far-off object who, every five minutes, is going to make a "significant" contribution by shaking my head vertically and saying, "Uh-huh. Uh-huh." I am going to be an active participant in therapy. Together we are going to work on whatever the present problem might be. And if we are going to take the time to be honest with each other, to share our thoughts and feelings, our hidden frustration and hurts and anger, then I have to be brave enough to accept their feelings and lay the groundwork for constructive, helpful advice.

This kind of a relationship is necessary before a psychologist and his client can begin to work on the problem. How much more important is it that we open up and show our emotions to our mates, and that we accept his or her emotions without feeling threatened or without being judgmental?

For us to be successful in therapy, in life, in marriage, we must really learn to trust each other. Most of the time trust is not defined properly. When we think of trust within a marital relationship we believe our mate will be faithful. When your husband is out to a business meeting, you know that he is not up to "monkey business," chasing a barmaid around some dimly lit bar. That isn't trust, my friends. Trust is telling the other person who you really are, sharing those most intimate thoughts and feelings. It's a little bit like our friends from Allstate. Here are my feelings within my cupped hands; I'm going to share them with you because I know you will treat my feelings with kid gloves. You're not going to roll over me, castigate me or push my feelings aside. That's really what trust is all about—giving emotional support to the other person, knowing that you can venture out to do that.

Our goal should be to give pleasure and not inflict pain.

You can train a little two-year-old to jump into Daddy's arms. You start just a foot away and let the child jump safely into Daddy's arms. By increasing the distance between parent and child you could train that two-year-old to jump from almost any height as long as Daddy always continued to catch him. That is what we need to do in marriage. We need a *childlike faith* that we can trust the one we love with our feelings. Then we can venture out of darkness and into the light of a deep, caring relationship.

In summary, sharing our feelings with each other is not a one-shot deal. It's a continual process of unraveling the mystery of each of us to the other. Every day we're changing, we're perceiving different things. We have different attitudes and we must talk over these changes.

Begin today to share your feelings. Listen for the words that might indicate that you are blaming someone else for your feelings. If and when that happens, realize it, express it, retreat, gather your thoughts and feelings again and then go forward. It's not going to be a rose garden. It's not going to be a 180-degree difference; but if you begin to plod through the various thoughts and feelings you have, you'll find that your relationship experiences a new high, a new awareness of a love that once was, or should be. *Acceptance* is what happens after you have shared your feelings.

Notes
1. Genesis 1:27,31.
2. Ephesians 4:26.
3. H. Norman Wright, *The Pillars of Marriage* (Ventura, CA: Regal Books, 1979), pp. 156,157.

SEVEN

How to Be Good and Angry

One of the best sermons I ever heard in my life was delivered by our pastor, John Lovgren. It was entitled, "How to Be Good and Angry." The title says a lot to me. It indicates that anger is OK when it is dealt with in a responsible fashion.

We have a right to be angry. Like other emotions, which we discussed in the previous chapter, anger is not "right" or "wrong." Anger is just another emotion. However, in order for us to begin to deal with the concept of anger we must realize that while we do have the right to get mad at certain acts or incidents, we don't have the right to inflict injury on anyone else because of our anger. Again, the key is whether we express anger toward the *act* or toward the *individual.* For example, the father can say, "I am really angry that this milk shake is spilled all over the car seat, but I can get a rag and clean it up." This way he is not denying the fact of his anger but is finding a satisfactory solution to his feelings (cleaning up the spill with the rag). More importantly, his three-year-old, who just made the colossal mess, will not be made to feel guilty. Your anger is directed toward the "goop" and not toward your little son or daughter.

Most of us have never really dealt with anger. We have been taught to turn anger inward, toward ourselves, keeping our real feelings inside. Then, in pressure-cooker fashion, the hurts, feelings, and frustrations begin to boil to the surface. We "blow" and our anger becomes destructive because it lashes out at anyone who is unfortunate enough to be in our path. Too often, the recipients of this anger are the ones we love the most.

I find in counseling other people that, in marriage, anger is often accentuated after the bedroom door closes. Forty-one year old Nadine complained that every time she turned around, her husband was getting "frisky." Bob, 43, defended himself by saying that he couldn't help it if he had a strong sexual drive. Moreover he made his wife feel guilty for not always being submissive to him. The truth was that Bob was a very angry person. He had never learned to communicate with Nadine and was fearful of telling her how insecure he felt. He controlled his feelings of inadequacy by his seemingly macho, aggressive and insatiable sexual appetite.

For years Nadine avoided Bob, faked it, invented excuses—but Bob's hunger for sex continued. In counseling Nadine, I told her that she was missing the boat; it wasn't so much the sex that Bob wanted from her, it was continual reaffirmation of his dominance over her. He showed it sexually. You should have seen the surprised look on Nadine's face when I suggested that she not only submit *every* time Bob approached her for sex, but that she also go the extra mile and initiate the act! In spite of her amazement, Nadine took my suggestion. As she began to chase after Bob, he became bewildered and unsure of their changing relationship. The more she pushed, the more he began to withdraw into a shell.

Within 60 days of applying this action-oriented method Nadine's husband became *impotent!* Since Bob was no longer successful at dominating her in an aggressive manner he turned to passive means (impotency) to control and dominate Nadine. (It's just as controlling to be impotent as it is to be overly aggressive.)

Suppressed Anger

I am going to borrow H. Norman Wright's outline that describes how we usually respond to anger. He says that (1) we suppress it, (2) we express it, (3) we repress it, or (4) we confess it.[1] Bob is an example of a person who *suppressed his anger.* Someone who suppresses anger knows he is angry but doesn't know what to do about it. He keeps it under wraps, hidden from the world. But eventually it has to spill out, and when it does it comes in uncontrolled actions or words. Bob's anger vented itself in controlling his wife. He manifested it by continually demanding sex from her.

Expressed Anger

The person who *expresses anger* is the one who shows his well-developed temper. He is a controller, so he lets loose and tells by his action that he is angry and everybody better pay attention. Notice the next time someone throws a temper tantrum, whether a child or an adult. It's like "E.F. Hutton is talking!" Everyone stops to listen. The one who expresses anger is telling people to keep back, to keep in their place; "you're getting too close to my real self."

Many think of temper as an emotion that has been with us since day one, some kind of disease that we have been endowed with. There is some evidence to support the theory that people are born with certain temperaments. I haven't found that to be true in my private practice. My experience has been that when a person gains insight into his temper, the temper dissipates into thin air; it often loses its purposeful nature once we have disclosed the psychological payoffs for the behavior. In essence it lifts a heavy burden from the person when he can understand how he uses his temper in his relationship with others.

I had a surgeon as a client several years ago. In conversation in my office he appeared to be shy and withdrawn. It was only after I visited his wife that I found out that this "shy person" punched holes in the walls of his home with his fist. He became terribly explosive when the littlest thing went wrong. He was a controller, but while he was able to keep it "under control" in one area, he wasn't in the other.

Sometimes shyness can be a means of controlling—or expressing anger. Notice a situation when several children come into a room. (Maybe at a children's party or at church nursery). One of the children will invariably take a step backwards and act as if he doesn't want to join the group. Usually the adult in the room will make a special effort to go over and talk to little "Snooky" about joining the group. The psychological dynamics of that situation is that the child is saying, "Hey! I'm very powerful. I don't come like everyone else. I need a special invitation and escort." In going over and trying to induce the child to join the group the adult is doing just the opposite of what he or she should be doing. If the child chooses not to be in the group, let him stay out for awhile. The natural consequence for not joining the group will be missing out on a special activity, or the ice cream and cake. Going over and giving special audience is convincing the child that his assumption that he only counts in life when he is in control of other people is a right assumption.

Repressed Anger

Many times I see people in counseling sessions who have become depressed. Often depression is a result of bottling up anger, of *repressing it*. Norm Wright believes that many Christians repress anger because they honestly think that because they know Christ they are not supposed to become angry, that anger is not a legitimate emotion for them.[2]

When you deal with anger by repressing it you are trying not to admit to anyone that you are angry or that you feel anger. Because you have never learned to express anger in a constructive manner, repression takes its toll. Let me give you an idea of how tricky repression, and the resulting depression, is and how important it is that you show your feelings—both positive and negative—openly with each other.

Something happens to provoke anger in you. Because you don't know better you repress it. Repressed anger is tucked away. Soon it begins to simmer and boil deep inside you. This simmering may have begun in childhood because your parents wouldn't allow you to be angry. So if there is no place for this anger to go, it turns inward. Eventually you become depressed.

Depression can *serve a purpose in a person's life.*

Although we think of depression in the negative sense, it is really productive behavior for the one who fears sharing his real self and real feelings with his mate. Depression may be used to get back at one's mate for perceived mistreatment within a marriage. It may be a way of keeping someone over the proverbial barrel. Depression can be a crying out for someone to become involved and close. A person might choose to become depressed at a subconscious level. If one's mate is thinking about leaving, the rejected mate might very well become depressed as a way of keeping the mate. The logic might go something like this: "How can you even think of leaving me now that I'm depressed and so hurt. If you leave, I'll kill myself." Instead of dealing with the anger that caused the depression the person tries to make the mate feel guilty so he or she cannot possibly leave.

Lewis, a dentist, was a highly successful and respected person within the community. He was very much devoted to his work, a perfectionist (like most dentists), who had the innate capability of keeping people at arm's length at all cost. This meant he could never open up to anyone, to share his emotions—including anger. His wife was no different from others—she couldn't get close to him either. She started a business of her own and was gradually becoming financially and emotionally independent of him. As she got more free of him, his depression increased to such a degree that he could no longer function on a daily basis—he was repressing his anger.

Lewis had diagnosed himself (like most professionals) as a chronic depressive. He thought psychotherapy might be of some assistance. As I listened to his tale of woe, I realized that his depression was probably purposive behavior; he seemed uptight as he explained his situation. I could see that his depression was his way of telling his wife, "You can't leave me, particularly when I'm down." It was his final effort to keep her knuckled under. When I disclosed to him the psychological, purposeful nature of his depression, it began to lift like a fog on a warm summer morning. Unfortunately, his repressed anger and his perfectionistic tendencies and his need to keep people at arm's length were too deep-seated. He paid dearly for his inability to share his emotions. His wife grew tired of the relationship, in which she gave and received very little in return, and finally went her own way.

Confessed Anger

The best way to handle anger is to *confess it* before it gets out of control or is tucked away. But be careful how you confess it. As in other emotions we have a tendency to blame the other person for our anger. I remember a student in one of my counseling classes who told me that his wife made him angry. I queried him, "Now, Peter, where does the anger come from?" He said, "It comes from my wife." I told him that was impossible, "The anger can't pass from your wife into yourself. You create, manufacture, and distribute your own anger. Your cop-out is telling me that she makes you angry. But you make yourself angry. You choose to be angry on the basis of what you select out and hear. You have a choice of dealing with your emotions. You can choose anger, patience, understanding or violence. You're going to be held accountable either way."

Instead of pointing to others and saying, "Hey! You make me angry!" you should learn to say, "Hey! I feel angry about this situation." Dr. David Augsburger suggests that when you find yourself using another person or "'it' as an explanation or a scapegoat, stop. Listen to yourself. Recognize what you're doing: avoiding responsibility; sidestepping the real problem; denying ownership of your feelings, responses, and actions. . . . My actions are mine. Your actions are yours. I am responsible for my behavior. You are responsible for yours."[3]

Of course confessing anger in this way comes after you have answered the question, "Can I share it with my mate?" If we can get to a point where we begin to share anger and frustration with each other in a positive way, then we are beginning to put together a marriage. It doesn't make any difference what the source of the anger is. Many times the anger may have been precipitated by something that happened earlier in the day or the week. Maybe your boss asked you to do something that you didn't really feel comfortable doing. You couldn't say, "Hey boss, I really don't want to do that!" So the anger got displaced into your home. The people you love the most, your wife and children, became the dumping ground for your frustration and anger.

David Augsburger, in his book *Be All That You Can Be*, tells how you can make the most of your anger. "Anger is a vital, valid, natural emotion. As an emotion, it is in itself neither right nor wrong. The rightness or wrongness depends on the way it is released and exercised.

"Be angry, but be aware. You are never more vulnerable than when in anger. Self-control is at an all-time low, reason decreases, common sense usually forsakes you.

"Be angry, but be aware that anger quickly turns bitter, it sours into resentment, hatred, malice, and even violence unless it is controlled by love.

"Be angry, but only to be kind. Only when anger is

motivated by love of your brother, by love of what is right for people, by what is called from you by the love for God, is it constructive, creative anger.

"Make the most of your anger. Turn it from selfish defensiveness to selfless compassion."[4]

How can we deal with anger? We deal with anger by replacing it with an act of love. For example, it's late Saturday morning. You wife is still in the rack. You've been puttering around the house and suddenly make a decision, "SHE ought to be up." You're angry. You stomp in and say, "You ought to be up. It's ten o'clock!" This is not the way to get Saturday off on the right foot.

Suppose you choose to be loving, not ornery. If you know your wife's needs and know her feelings and are sensitive to them, you'll get your tail out into the kitchen. Make her a cup of coffee; bring it to her bedside and rub her back softly. Yes, you're still angry. You're not really happy that she's still in bed, but the question is, do you love her and do you want to meet her needs? If you do, you'll put your needs on the back court of life and you'll service her needs. Waking her up with a back rub and a cup of coffee is going to make this Saturday a great day for both of you. Everything is more effective when it's done in love and not in anger. *Love really is a daily decision.*

Action, Not Words

Whenever you feel that there are some angry thoughts to be shared, why don't you and your mate take a bath together? I know that sounds absolutely crazy. Plunge in! Sit facing each other in the bathtub. This is probably the best environment within a home to fight—it's very difficult to get up and run to the next room and close the door. This setting also removes all barriers from both of you. But be sure to keep the rules in mind: (1) you have a right to be angry; (2) you express anger at the *act* not at the person; (3) verbalize your anger, (4) listen to the other person without thinking what you are going to say in defense; (5) be sure to be specific; (6) ask your mate how he or she would like you to be different, or how you can change your behavior; (7) be sure to find a satisfactory solution to the anger.

Most of us who experience anxiety and anger within our lives are angry about things that happened in the past—"bone-digging" again. We are rarely dealing with the here and now. We might even be worried and anxious about the future. Remember what Jesus said, "Do not worry about tomorrow, for tomorrow will worry about itself. Each day has enough trouble of its own."[5] The fact is that you have X amount of psychological energy in your life. The choice you have to make is, "How do I want to use my energy?" Worrying about everything? Becoming angry at "things"? When you're worried or angry, there's no room to love, because worry is all-consuming. Your energy is being wasted on the negative.

I often think that some people seem to be in the center of a big pool, treading water. They aren't making any progress in any direction in their lives. They're just treading water. That really is the psychological plight of thousands. They don't go one way or the other. They stay in the middle and feel safe; no commitments. In this "safe" position they don't have to make choices that life requires of them.

But the fact is, that if you stay treading water long enough in life, *you're going to drown.* You have to make a movement in a positive direction. If there is something that needs to be done in your life today, and you know that some movement is necessary and a decision has to be made, begin to work toward that end right now. The anxiety and anger will be lessened immediately when you begin to solve problems by decision-making.

Maybe you've never learned to communicate your emotions. You've never been taught; you've never had the opportunity of sharing yourself with others. Perhaps your self-worth is so beaten down by your mate or your family that you have just thrown in the towel and given up. No one has ever wanted to meet your needs. But recognize the fact that it is OK to be angry. When you verbally express—confess—your anger, sharing it with someone else, you are really committing an act of love—*if you feel angry toward the* act *and not toward* the *person.*

Begin to practice sharing with your mate now. Make a special time each day when you can have quality time together. You are going to have difficulties in your marriage, it isn't all going to be smooth; accept that fact. You are two individuals with different needs, wants and emotional levels. You won't always be feeling good at the same time, but it's at these times when you need to be understanding of your mate. If you are indifferent to your mate's emotions then you'd better check out your love clock and see if it's still ticking. Indifference breeds discontent.

Notes
1. H. Norman Wright, *Communication: Key to Your Marriage* (Ventura, CA: Regal Books, 1974), pp. 87-92.
2. Ibid., p. 90.
3. David Augsburger, *Caring Enough to Confront* (Ventura, CA: Regal Books, 1973), p. 46.
4. David Augsburger, *Be All You Can Be* (Carol Stream IL: Creation House, 1970), pp. 31,32.
5. Matthew 6:34.

EIGHT

Games Couples Play

Who's winning your marriage?

I've noticed that couples tend to play games with each other. Not nice, innocent, fun-loving games, but competitive games designed to conquer the other spouse. And these games usually manifest themselves in the bedroom or in our sexual relationship.

In this chapter I want to talk about a few of the more deadly games I've encountered from couples I've counseled in my private practice.

Kill the Umpire

The first game I call "Kill the Umpire." Kill the Umpire is really a neat game because it brings to the marriage a little rule book for living. This book lists all the rules for life-style and marriage which we have been compiling for years, the most rigid of which are the sexual expectations for ourselves and for others.

If a couple is a typical couple they never received any premarital counseling about sex, nor have they ever really spent a great deal of time talking with each other about sexual preferences. So in trial and error fashion they go into the marital relationship and begin to explore, to find out, to test. Now if the husband begins to violate the wife's moral code, or one of the rules in her rule book of life, she might get right into the game, Kill the Umpire, by saying, "Foul ball, Charlie. One more of those and you're out of the game."

It sounds amusing, but it's so true. If someone violates our rules we get angry, we do yell, "Foul!" and threaten to throw the other party out of the park; and of course there have been plenty of husbands who have spent the night on the couch because he violated one rule or another. Much of this kind of thing and he has the urge to "kill the umpire!"

The point is that we rarely share our personal rule books with our marriage partners. We don't talk to each other about certain things—about how we feel about sex, how we feel about each other; we just, at the appropriate time, yell, "Foul!" In counseling sessions I challenge couples to think about the fact that the marital bed *cannot be defiled* with each other. I tell them that what goes on between them behind closed doors is OK, alright, as long as it's not forced and is mutually agreed upon. (After all, love does not demand its own way.)

At one of my seminars I began to talk about oral sex. Out of the corner of my eye I saw a woman hit her husband in the ribs and say, "OK, Harvey, that did it. Come on, we're going home."

Old Harvey said to Marge, "Wait a minute, Marge. I want to hear what the man has to say."

This is a typical reaction to a topic such as oral sex. Many of us have come into marriage with very definite cement-like guidelines for proper and improper sexual behavior between man and wife.

I think the Scripture is very clear when it talks about the fact that a husband's body belongs to his wife and a wife's body belongs to her husband. For the two to really become one in marriage, there must be this melting together—this fulness, this oneness.

Now I'm not suggesting that each of us go out and incorporate oral sex into our marital relationship, but I'm using oral sex as a way to try to challenge you to think about the fact that most of us bring to marriage these mythical limits. But I've seen many couples transcend these mythical limits and reach a more satisfying marriage. There is nothing wrong or dirty in two people sharing each other sexually, as long as it's a loving, giving act. Our mission in marriage is to meet the other person's needs.

I do a lot of seminars in churches. Christians are perhaps in the most difficult position when it comes to enjoying their sexual relationships. This is probably because many of us were brought up in homes where it was conveyed that sex is bad; our genitals are bad; we are never supposed to touch each other or our own selves, or experience any kind of pleasure; no one ever talked about sex, therefore sex must be bad, etc. I spend more time undoing—particularly with married women—what well-meaning parents did to them when they were young kids, giving them tremendous hang-ups about sex.

Many of us as parents tell children that sex is "bad." But when a child begins to develop physically, when he is able to discover his own physical feelings by way of masturbation, you can imagine what the child's reaction might be, "Hey, this isn't so bad after all!" There is no sense in telling children in any way, shape or form that sex is bad. Sex is beautiful, sex is good, it is a God-given capability each of us has to enjoy. However, like any other privilege we have in life, it has guidelines that go along with it, restraints that must go with it. We can't just act out our feelings all the time.

It's important for us to realize that we must talk to people close to us about our sexuality in a positive way. Sexual feelings are OK, they're natural; kids should be taught at an early age that we have these feelings within us, that God has given us the capacity to feel, to experience.

Think back to the most pleasurable sexual experience you've ever had. That special time with your husband or your wife that was absolutely the greatest. Chances are it was a time when the foundation was laid for sex to take place. When the husband was loving from the beginning of the day until the end of day; when the husband felt prized and wanted and special. But chances are that special physical emotional time together just happened. It was a spontaneous loving moment.

Who gave us the abilities to experience that intense, emotional, physical feelings? I believe it was God. God gave man and wife the ability to experience the pleasures, the intimacies of each other. So as loving couples we have nothing to be ashamed of. We have nothing to be fearful of. It's OK for us to come together as one in marriage and to love each other.

For many of us who have had feelings of guilt associated with sex, it will take some time to work our way back to where

God wants us to be in our marriages. But it can be done. If both partners in a marriage don't work at becoming one, then the marriage may be threatened by still another game.

Take That, You Rat!

How many women have heard the story that her husband was "working late" or hear her husband say he is "too tired" or isn't interested in sex? Or how many husbands leave home not knowing that the mailman or the milkman is going to stop by for his daily visit after he leaves?

One kindly but dull husband found that his wife was greeting the mailman every day (the neighbors knew all about it but he was surprised when his wife asked for a divorce). It seems that it all started very innocently with a cup of coffee; before long the children were being sent out of the house when the mail truck stopped. These kinds of affairs not only destroy the marriage and are against all concepts of Christian morality, but they take their toll on the family in the example they set for the children.

It seemed like a pretty typical call. A prominent businessman in the community was calling for an appointment for himself and his wife. He told me on the phone that they had a few "minor communication" problems and thought that perhaps some professional assistance might help them sort things out. He insisted, however, that he meet with me first. I told him that wasn't the way I usually worked but I would defer to his better judgment.

Ed was a tremendously successful businessman but, more than that, he was very much wrapped up in his work as an elder within his church. As he described his heavy commitment to his activities within his church I found it hard to believe that he had time to devote to his business, which was flourishing so much under his direction. As he spoke of his wife, he did so with a sense of pride; he described Kathy as beautiful, warm-hearted, very capable, a good mom and a good wife but somewhat "immature." As I pressed him for what he meant by immature, he explained that she was not very understanding of his many commitments, particularly within the church and business community.

Ed further explained that recently there had been a number of petty issues that had mushroomed into various squabbles and he felt there was need for some "minor adjustment" within their marriage. By now it was evident that Ed and Kathy had a competitive marriage.

When I met Kathy at our second session, I noticed several instances which pointed out that both Ed and Kathy had a great deal of interest in proving who was right. And again, if someone is right in a relationship, then someone has to be wrong. Somebody wins, somebody loses!

I felt the need to have the next appointment with Kathy alone. In classical fashion, five minutes before the end of our session she dropped the bomb. She said, "Well, I suppose if this is going to do any good, I'd better tell you the truth." I was about ready for anything at that point, and I had a sneaking suspicion I was going to hear that there was some-one else in Kathy's life. Boy! Was I right!

Kathy was having an affair with someone in the church, right under her "elder" husband's nose and he didn't even know it. (Take that, you rat!) He was so busy and so totally absorbed in the church that he neglected to take seriously his first responsibility as a husband (to meet his wife's every need). If he had, she would never have sought out an affair.

It was interesting that when Kathy described Paul to me (the gentleman she was having the affair with), she described him in terms that would indicate that he was easy to talk to and that he was a listener. He took the time to listen to what Kathy thought and felt. He *valued* what she said. Comparing that with Ed's style, it wasn't difficult to see why Paul was so attractive to Kathy.

As we began to go back into Kathy's life at our next session she gradually developed a greater trust and ability to be open with me. She shared with me that she had two prior affairs, all within the church, all right under her husband's nose, so to speak. Kathy felt very guilty about her affairs, yet at this point I felt there was a need to show her that there were some logical reasons for her to seek out an affair. I am not saying that an affair is ever right, but when someone is having an affair there is a reason for it, something we can learn from the incident. Whatever needs are being met in the affair are usually the same needs that are neglected within the marriage.

Kathy felt that she only counted in life when she was being noticed, when everyone was paying attention to her. This was an almost neurotic need in her life. And in what job was her husband doing the absolute worst? That of paying some attention to his beautiful and talented wife. If he had only done his homework she would never have sought out an affair.

Kathy was tormented about whether or not to share this information with her husband. I told her that in this case I thought it was best that she confess her affairs to God and then bury them. At the same time she could make a new commitment to her husband. I knew her confession to her husband would create undue stress on their relationship. Her outpouring of guilt might be only a dumping on her husband, and it might be something he wouldn't be able to handle.

Ed and Kathy finally got it together with the help of a beautiful 44-hour weekend, Marriage Encounter! Kathy decided to confess her shortcomings to God and to bury her affairs once and for all. In order to do this she had to approach the three men with whom she had affairs. She asked for forgiveness from each of them and at the same time forgave them! This action on her part alleviated much of the guilt she had within her. By way of a great weekend (Marriage Encounter) she and Ed made new commitments to each other to always put each other's needs first. They closed their weekend by repeating the marriage vows while in each other's arms.

Marriage Encounter is offered through the Lutheran, Methodist, Catholic, Jewish and other faiths. I recommend it to interested couples who have a good marriage. It is not recommended as therapy for deeply troubled marriages; marriage counseling is still the best route to go for these. A few phone calls to area churches should get you in touch with a Marriage Encounter seminar in your area.

Action, Not Words

Every once in a while it is a good idea to take a look at your marriage vows and repeat them to each other. With your arms around each other repeat the following vows (or the one you used for your wedding) as you look into each other's eyes.

"I (your name) take thee (your mate's name) to be my wedded wife/husband; to have and to hold from this day forward, for better or for worse, for richer or poorer, in sickness and in health, to love, honor and cherish till death do us part, according to God's holy Word."

Who's winning your marriage? If one of you is winning then the other is losing, and where does that put your marriage and the oneness it is supposed to attain? Remember, you're on the same team!

Dump Truck

Another game I see in too many marriages I call "Dump Truck." Now this is really a combative game and a very destructive one. Picture yourself and your mate each owning your own little dump truck. You park your dump truck under your side of the bed. Both dump trucks are appropriately filled with steer manure. The game goes like this: every time you feel that your mate has violated one of your rules you get into your little dump truck, put it in reverse and back it toward your mate. Then push the little button. The tailgate opens up and the trailer lifts and the steer manure is dumped on your mate. As he or she begins to push away the steer manure, the thinking might very well be at that point, "OK, if you have the right to dump on me, guess what right I have? That's right. To dump on you." So the other mate climbs in the dump truck and retaliates.

This dumping process is a continual one and is usually done on a one-for-one basis. Many times I see couples who have gone through this dumping process over a long period of time, then when they reach down to try to feel something toward their mates they come up empty. And my comment is usually along the line of, "Yeah, I can see why you wouldn't feel anything. Does it have anything to do with the fact that you've got 16 cubic yards of steer manure covering your relationship?"

You cannot win in a marriage if you're competing with each other. You can't make it in life as a married couple if you have a competitive relationship. In time it will prove to be destructive. If you and your marital partner have been in the habit of dumping on each other, now is the time to make a commitment to change your habits before your marriage relationship sinks to the depth that Katie's and Ron's had.

Katie was noticeable in that her five-foot-four-inch frame carried 247 pounds. She and her six-foot-three-inch, 155 pound husband had come to me for marital therapy. You could always tell when Katie and Ron were coming into the office because a string of four-letter words would emerge from the parking lot below. They took the prize in the game Dump Truck. They were in the worst shape of any couple I had ever seen professionally. In their three-and-a-half year marriage Katie had had 12 affairs that she could at least attach a name to, and numerous one-night stands whose names somehow escaped her. These affairs weren't the results of neglect, they were Katie's way of dumping.

Katie, 25, was a very powerful woman. On many occasions she had put her fist through the plasterboard walls in her home. While she tended to be explosive, her husband was passive. What was it someone once said about opposites attracting?

Occasionally, in therapy, clients get the idea that the therapist is pitting one mate against the other. One evening Katie thought I was doing just that. She became very angry, called me a nasty name, and proceeded to leave the office in a huff, slamming the door behind her. She was going to walk home (even though she lived eight miles from the office) to show both of us that she was the boss. She wanted us to know that we had made her feel uncomfortable, guilty, and we were going to pay!

Ron immediately sprang to his feet to chase after Katie. I literally grabbed him by the seat of his pants and told him to sit down. I asked, "Ron, is this typical? Is this the kind of thing that goes on in the home?"

"Yes," he replied, "she's always doing this, throwing tantrums of one kind or another."

I assured him that if things were going to turn around in his marriage, he had better begin by behaving differently. "So let's start right now," I advised. "Rather than chasing Katie down and telling her you're sorry, let her walk home."

Katie left the office like a steamroller with a full head of steam. She took off, waddling down the street, determined to walk home. In the back of her mind she probably *knew* Ron wouldn't be too far behind, ready to bring her home again and patch things up with an apology and a little sex for good measure.

At an intersection about a mile away from the office something happened to Katie—she entered into an abyss! She fell into a construction hole and broke her leg in two places. She lay there until approximately 2:30 A.M. when someone finally heard her cry for help. The fire-rescue paramedics came and took her to a hospital for emergency treatment.

Her husband, home hours earlier, had already gone to bed for the night. In the early hours of dawn he answered the telephone. The nurse on the other end essentially said that his wife had had an accident; she had broken her leg and was asking if he could please come to the emergency room right away. Ron reflexively replied that he would be there in just a few minutes. After he hung up he began to wonder, "What would Leman suggest?" So rather than get dressed and go down to the emergency room, he simply rolled over and went back to sleep.

The next morning at 10:00 Ron sauntered into Katie's hospital room. Her first words were, "When I get out of here I'm going to break your little neck!" But, you know, to this day Katie maintains that this particular incident was the event that triggered lasting behavioral changes in their marriage.

You might be getting the idea that Katie was the "bad guy" in this Dump Truck game. But such was not the case. Remember, Dump Truck is a two-person game. *Fighting is an act of cooperation.* It does take two to disco. Ron's favorite dumping was using a large vocabulary which he *knew* Katie wouldn't understand. Ron had a two-year college degree, Katie an eighth grade education. He seemingly enjoyed the instances when Katie appeared confused and ignorant! She handled those "put-downs" by way of the many affairs she had. Her private logic was, "OK, if you have the right to put me down and make me feel bad then I have the right to get back at you." Revenge is usually a two-edged sword, hurting self and others through striking out.

What can we learn from Ron and Katie?

First, when we change our behavior it forces our partner to take a good hard look at the relationship. If you and your mate have been playing Dump Truck for a while then it's time for one of you, if not both, to care enough to take some action toward change. The most dangerous signal that your marriage is in trouble is when you simply *don't care* one way or another about what is taking place in your relationship.

Ron and Katie's marriage shows how important it is to make a commitment to *change*. But you can *never* change your partner; you cannot stop the alcoholic from taking a drink; you cannot stop the over-indulgent eater; *you cannot make another adult do anything!* The change and commitment must start from within your own self. Ron and Katie were miles apart emotionally but they made the decision to seek therapy together. Ron's commitment to remove his sails from Katie's wind by doing the unexpected was the action needed to precipitate change.

Where does a marriage counselor begin in a marriage as seemingly hopeless as Ron and Katie's? I asked them if they ever stopped fighting, if they ever stopped dumping on each other. Ron spoke up and said, "Yeah! during and after sex!"

"Fine, then we're going to start there."

Ron asked, "Where?"

I said, "Right there. In your home when you're having sex. The next time you are in that position I want you to just hold each other while praying aloud, thanking the good Lord for your crummy relationship." We had to start someplace!

Realizing that even beautiful cathedrals are built one brick at a time, Ron and Katie began to build their relationship toward a real marriage.

A very special picture hangs in my office and will probably be with me the rest of my life. After several months of intensive therapy, Katie and Ron came back to me. They handed me the picture and Katie told me, "Dr. Leman, this is for your office. I want you to think of us when other couples come for help. Feel free to tell them our story."

They were really beautiful in their new "coupleness." They had just come from Montgomery Ward where they had bought a new set of dishes. This was symbolic and special for them in that they had literally broken every dish in their house, throwing them at each other. (Back in the kitchen again?!) Finally, they were friends and lovers, as well as sexual partners. Katie had lost 100 pounds over an eight-month period with the help of Weight Watchers. She had made a number of changes physically as the inner Katie changed.

Ron and Katie had learned many things the hard way. Isn't that true of most of us? That reminds me of the story of the lion, the donkey, and the fox who went on a rampage throughout the jungle, killing everything in sight. After a two-and-a-half-hour killing spree the lion decided it was time to rest. The lion asked the donkey to divide the prey fairly among the three. After the donkey completed his work by dividing the prey into three equal parts, the lion became enraged and clawed the donkey to death and ate him.

The lion then turned to the fox and said, "Mr. Fox, would you please divide the prey fairly?" The sly old fox went over and took a mangy bird and put it in front of himself while he moved all the rest of the game in front of the lion. The curious lion looked at the fox and said, "Mr. Fox! Where did you learn to divide so fairly and so evenly?"

The fox looked up and said, "The donkey taught me."

It's true, isn't it? Many of us as husbands, wives and lovers learn the hard way.

Action, Not Words

To find out if you and your mate are playing Dump Truck

in your marriage, try playing another game, "Marital Base-ball." Make three columns on a piece of paper. At the top of the first column write "Innings." Underneath, number down from 1 to 7 (seven innings in this baseball game, one for each day in a week). At the top of the other two columns put an H (for husband) and W (for wife). Tape your baseball scorecard on the refrigerator door. Every time either of you dumps on your mate give yourself a score—one, two or three runs each inning. If you haven't scored all day, give yourself a big goose egg. I think you'll find at the end of the week that the score is pretty even. Most couples who have competitive marriages compete on an almost even keel.

Children Are the Enemy

The first time I heard a psychologist say, "Children are the enemy," I thought to myself, "Oh boy, here's another wacko psychologist making another off-the-wall remark about children." At that time I didn't have any children. I have since learned to savor those words: Children *are* the enemy.

This game pits not you against your spouse, but you and your mate against those darling little "gifts of the Lord."[1] It's played in some homes something like this: There you are in your living room, just you and your partner. You finally got the children in bed, now it's time for some quiet talk between the two of you. However, you made one fatal assumption: that the children are tucked away for the night. Thirty feet away, unknown to you, your 11-year-old and 10-year-old have taken three-and-a-half year old Herbie into confidence. "Herbie, Herbie. You go out there and tell Mom and Dad you're hungry and you want something to eat. Go on, get out there. Scoot." Little Herbie begins to shuffle his feet toward the living room, blankey in tow. He's so cute—he looks just like your father. But your first instinct when you see that little spittin' image out of his bed is—KILL HIM!

But you don't kill him. Most of us as parents say, "OK, one quick snack and right into bed." Before we get the words out of our mouths, two more shadows appear down the hallway. Score: children 1, parents 0. Children are the enemy!

Or you and your spouse are sitting together on the couch, immensely enjoying the quiet. Suddenly—thump, bump, scrape, and "aaauuughhh!" from your seven-year-old son. That's Dad's cue to jump up and storm toward their bedroom. He snatches the door nearly off its hinges and shouts, "OK, who started it?" The kids, of course, in complete cooperation, point to each other. With a "this is the *last* time I'm going to tell you. Go to sleep," Dad slams the bedroom door. Once the door is closed, the little angels look at each other, grinning from ear to ear. The oldest, with his hand over his mouth, stage whispers, "Didya see his face? Didya ever see anything so red? I never saw his veins pop out that far." Score another one for the kids.

Children are the enemy. Anything that comes between us as husband and wife is the enemy, even though most of us feel that our children are very special to us and that we love them very much. Now, realizing that children are the enemy, it behooves us to keep watch for the ways they can launch an assault against us so that we can have our defenses ready. I've been able to isolate several areas in family life where children are likely to attack, weakening the foundations of our marriage. I will talk about four of these areas in this book.

First, we tend to live our lives through our children. Children no longer see themselves as social unequals; they see themselves very much equal to us as adults in every respect. Everything we do, 24 hours a day is regulated by the children. We fix our meals when they want to eat, and we serve what they like; we see the TV programs they want to see; we plan our free time around their schedule; we allow them to monopolize conversation.

It is very easy for us to let our children take too much energy and time from our relationship with each other. They demand so much time that we even have guilt feelings when we leave them with a sitter for an evening. To get away for a weekend seems an enormous violation of responsibility toward them. But, as I have said repeatedly in this book, it is necessary for Mommy and Daddy to get away alone for occasional weekends—and leave the enemy at home. This is not only a means to save the marriage, but it is also teaching your children that you place a very high premium on your special time together. It's a beautiful way to show children that your marriage comes first.

Second, we let them monopolize our time. When Dad comes home from work at 6:00, they all run to him with hugs and kisses, anxious to tell him all about their day. The wise parent, after giving the loves and kisses and greetings, will ask for some time out for just a few minutes to wind down. Then the time he spends with his children, even if it's only a few minutes before dinner, will at least be productive time. The wife needs to help her husband protect that necessary winding-down time. Also the mother who spends all day at home with her children must be sure to get away occasionally during the day. If Dad takes the initiative to make sure Mom has the dollars to get a baby-sitter and go out to lunch with a girlfriend, he helps her protect time for herself. If Mother also happens to be working all day, she usually doesn't get to punch out until 10:00 P.M. while Dad checks out of the family after the evening meal; the old double standard at work. (Incidentally, have you ever heard Dad tell some of the "boys" that he had to "baby-sit" with the kids, but when Mom does it, hour after hour, she's just fulfilling her role as a mother?)

Third, we allow them to determine our sex life. One question I am frequently asked at seminars is, "How do other couples find privacy for their sex life?" It was easy when the kids were little, but when they get older and have more time to themselves, there is an increasing possibility of interruptions of the parents' time together.

I remember one very rotund lady at a seminar who shared a very funny true story. She and her husband were enjoying themselves in the bedroom, making love. In the process they fell out of bed onto the floor. It made a terrible crash. The teenagers ran to the bedroom to investigate the frightening noise and there, in all their glory, were Mom and Dad, naked as jaybirds, on the floor. You know who was angry? The kids. They were upset because Mom and Dad didn't have the foresight to lock the door! They were angry because their parents didn't take the necessary steps to protect their privacy.

Many married people are very self-conscious about making love while their children are awake. They're deathly afraid that the children might hear loving sounds coming from the bedroom. I suggest that you turn up the stereo or tape deck to such a volume that it would cover any sounds;

of course they may accuse you, for a change, of playing *your* music too loud.

If one or both of you really feel uncomfortable about making love when the kids are in the house and awake, what's wrong with taking a motel room for an evening? Sounds almost romantic, doesn't it?

Several couples I have counseled have responded to my seed planting by going to a spa, a hot-tub resort, or a motel in their own city or in a nearby city for the night. Sure it costs dollars and it takes cooperation, but what a neat way to start putting romance back in your marriage. I remember traveling with my wife on a business trip. All of a sudden an amorous feeling got the best of me. We stopped at a motel (mid-day). On the way up the steps to the lobby we began to laugh and howl. We didn't have any luggage with us. My wife, to make herself feel more "legitimate," went back to the car and got her little plastic knitting bag to carry in with us. Somehow it made her feel better, but I wondered what anybody who happened to be watching thought.

Some might feel that spending money on a motel room is too frivolous, they think you should be able to control your emotions until you can have some privacy at home. But it's a lot more fun to stop, get away and take the time to enjoy each other. Life is too short for it to be the hassle it is for too many of us in marriage. We really have to live it one day at a time, and get the most out of it, enjoying each other. We can't plan on tomorrow. I can't think of a better investment than to invest in your relationship with your marital partner.

Part of the teaching we are responsible for is to teach our children about marital sex. It's important for your children to realize that Mommy and Daddy love each other and sex is a part of their love and of their life. It's important for us to communicate to our children that the sexual feelings they will have are natural and normal. If we convey to our children that sexual feelings are OK, then they will become brave enough to communicate with us their feelings about sex.

Let's face it. Talking about sex is very difficult and the best way to handle it is to keep the avenues open for relating our first-hand experiences to our children. I realize that what I am advising is very foreign to most of you, but if you open up and share with your children, you give them permission to share with you. Children will either learn sex from you in a healthy, marriage-related manner or they will learn it someplace else, possibly in a filthy manner.

Children should not be the enemy in our sexual life with each other.

Fourth, we let them divide and conquer. Children are very sensitive to any division there might be between you and your mate. When they discover a little light between you, they exert pressure to wedge you apart, creating animosity. I urge you to develop couple power, or your children will take advantage of any little differences you and your spouse may have.

Notice how many times children will aggravate a situation to get you and your mate at each other's throats? And it works. Why? Because you haven't come together as one in your marriage. You aren't seen by your children as an entity, as a couple. Let your children see that you are united. If issues come up—and they will—where you have different feelings about how matters should be handled, go behind closed doors and discuss it. Then come out, united, and give the children a decision. This is one reason why I advocate to parents that children have a very definite bedtime. Then when the children are in bed, we as adults can have time to ourselves to talk, to communicate about any differences we have, to prepare our strategy, if you please.

A word about set bedtimes. If your children are older they still should have a set time to go into their bedrooms. Do they have to be sleeping? No, but they have to be in their rooms; when they choose to go to bed is their business. The rule in my house is that children are to be in their rooms at a specified time so that my wife and I can have our very special time together.

One area where children often are able to divide and conquer is in the area of discipline. Jay Kesler, in his book, *Too Big to Spank,* has this to say about discipline: "To be united in our approach to rules and discipline provides a sense of confidence. Teens become unsure and apprehensive if they do not have guidelines. If they sense we are agreed and unified they are spared the insecurity of too much freedom. . . . Our experience has been that when we are not careful in the mutual understanding of rules we tend to have arguments. An agreement ahead of time is the best way to avoid misunderstanding later."[2]

If united discipline is not now practiced in your household, a good time to launch such a program is during the dinner hour when you are all together. The attitude for this tactic is arbitration. Explain that you feel it is necessary that some house rules be established so that everyone will understand where he stands. Get some input from your kids as to what rules ought to be instituted in the family. This kind of meeting where everybody gets a chance to pitch in and have input is the democratic way. Problems can be hashed out

and solved in a very logical and straightforward manner;
much better than if Mommy and Daddy talk it over and make
all the decisions. In this way you have a better chance of
winning the enemy over to your side.

Some of the family decisions, in addition to discipline
problems and house rules, that can be discussed in family
meetings are: where you spend your vacation together next
summer; who does what chores, or the reassigning of chores;
any conflict between family members.

Sometimes parents *make* enemies of their children by
being impatient, too restrictive, or inconsiderate of them. In
my book, *Parenthood Without Hassles* (*Well Almost),* I
gave a child's point of view of the parent-child relationship in
the form of Ten Commandments. These commandments
were picked up and repeated in the Dear Abby syndicated
newspaper column. Read them through and see if you have
made children your enemy in your home.

"1. My hands are small; please don't expect perfection
whenever I make a bed, draw a picture, or throw a ball. My
legs are short; please slow down so that I can keep up with
you.

"2. My eyes have not seen the world as yours have;
please let me explore safely: don't restrict me unnecessarily.

"3. Housework will always be there. I'm only little for
such a short time—please take time to explain things to me
about this wonderful world, and do so willingly.

"4. My feelings are tender; please be sensitive to my
needs; don't nag me all day long. (You wouldn't want to be
nagged for your inquisitiveness.) Treat me as you would like
to be treated.

"5. I am a special gift from God; please treasure me as

God intended you to do, holding me accountable for my actions, giving me guidelines to live by, and disciplining me in a loving manner.

"6. I need your encouragement, but not your praise, to grow. Please go easy on the criticism; remember, you can criticize the things I do without criticizing me.

"7. Please give me the freedom to make decisions concerning myself. Permit me to fail so that I can learn from my mistakes. Then someday I'll be prepared to make the kind of decisions life requires of me.

"8. Please don't do things over for me. Somehow that makes me feel that my efforts didn't quite measure up to your expectations. I know it's hard, but please don't try to compare me with my brother or my sister.

"9. Please don't be afraid to leave for a weekend together. Kids need vacations from parents, just as parents need vacations from kids. Besides, it's a great way to show us kids that your marriage is very special.

"10. Please take me to Sunday school and church regularly, setting a good example for me to follow. I enjoy learning more about God."[3]

Who's Number One?

I could probably describe several more destructive games which couples play against each other in a competitive marriage. Maybe you and your spouse are playing a game right now—one that I mentioned or one you thought up all by yourself. All "games" are threatening to your marriage, because if there is a "winner" then there has to be a "loser." And the "winner" becomes the loser, because he/she loses the whole marriage. What's important—winning your game or winning your marriage?

In the first chapter of the book I admonished you to put your marital partner Number One in your list of priorities. I have tried to reinforce that ideal all through the book. Let's do an exercise.

Action, Not Words

Each of you take a piece of paper and begin to rank, in order of importance to you (1 being most important), your own priorities in life, what is most important to you, next most important, and so on down the list to the least important. Make a list of at least 10 items. (Of course, God is primary on any list. This list begins after God.)

Next, list the way you see your mate's priorities for life. When you are finished compare your lists. What do they tell you about your relationship with each other? What things do you have to change? If your job is the most important thing in your life you are going to be unhappy in marriage. Big businesses are beginning to realize that the employee who puts his job before his home life is not as effective an employee as is the one who has a happy fulfilling marriage. Now I know that some of you are thinking, "Yeah, but you don't understand. My job is really important. In my line of work my job has to be number one in my life."

Baloney! Not to get you prematurely to your final resting place, but what would happen at your job if you died today? How long do you think it would be before your replacement could be where you left off? After they pass the hat in the office or make a donation to your favorite charity or the church building fund, or what have you, life goes on. Anyone who feels he is indispensable can get a rude awakening.

If your children are in the number one position, what is going to happen to your marriage when you find yourself in an empty nest, when the children have gone on to make their own lives and you and your marital partner are left alone to carry on your marriage?

You cannot put your husband or wife in the number two (or lower) position; your marital partner must be number one, your children number two. Your job should be number three at best.

I guarantee that if you put each other first in your marriage, if you know what *your* needs are and you know what *your mate's* needs are, and you both make a hundred percent effort to meet those needs, you're going to have a happy marriage. Your marriage is going to be fulfilling and rewarding for you in every respect. Your marriage is going to be the winner, and you'll never read *your* name in the divorce column of the daily newspaper.

Notes
1. See Psalm 127:3.
2. Jay Kesler, *Too Big to Spank* (Ventura, CA: Regal Books, 1978), pp. 66,67.
3. Kevin Leman, *Parenthood Without Hassles* (*Well, Almost)* (Eugene, OR: Harvest House Publishers, 1979), pp. 139, 140. Used by permission.

NINE

Ying-Yangs, Weenies, Tallywackers, and "The Thing"

People were still filing into the huge auditorium as I began to speak on the topic, "What Every Parent Ought to Know About Sex." After a very nice introduction and a warm reception I turned to the audience and the first words out of my mouth were, "What do we call penises in our society?"

Silence . . . dead silence! One lady in the front row elbowed her husband and seemed to ask him, "Harry, is he talking about piano players or what?"

I went right after them. "Come on, what do we call penises in our society? Better yet, what did your mother call your penis, men?" Finally, after not getting any response, I asked for a show of hands. I asked for suggestions. As I pointed to the audience, people began to yell out various terms: peter—weiner—pecker—pokey—the thing—ying-yang (a Chinese pecker?)—dork—dink—pee-wee—boy part—girl part . . . By this time the crowd was nearly hysterical. They were laughing, some so hard they were crying. They were about tearing up the place; but I went on and they continued to enjoy telling me their life secrets: ditty-wacker—tallywacker—ding-dong—pee-pee—tinker—tee-tee—shwantz—do-hickey—thing-a-majig—hooter . . . At this point I didn't even know if I was going to get through the evening.

What do these "cute," "funny" nicknames tell us about our feelings about sex? I believe this is a way we manifest our discomfort when we talk about sexual subjects. We have a very difficult time talking explicitly about sexual matters to each other as husbands and wives and to our children. Letha Scanzoni, in her book, *Sex Is a Parent Affair,* says that there is no reason "that a male toddler, who points to various parts of his body and hears his parents say, 'nose,' 'eye,' 'hand,' 'toe,' should suddenly hear strange euphemisms when he points to his genital area and hears 'pee-pee,' 'pee-wee,' 'wienie,' 'teapot,' 'periwinkle,' to cite only a few. Then he soon discovers that he is never to use the word around anyone outside the home. The correct name, of course, is *penis*, and the saclike structure under it is the *scrotum* and contains his *testicles*."[1]

Lack of Proper Sex Education

Most of us were taught early in childhood that sex was bad, dirty, and a subject that is never discussed in "nice" company. Think about your childhood. How did you learn about sex? Did you learn about it from a warm, open, loving discussion with your mom and dad, with them sitting down together and sharing part of their love life together with you? No! At some point in Junior's life Mom said to Dad, "You're going to have to talk to Junior about the birds and bees." And what did Dad do? He said, "Junior, Mother wants to talk to you about something!"

If you are a woman, during your preteen years, Mom or your gym teacher at school or your family doctor took just long enough to tell you about the advent of the monthly menstrual cycle. Of course, your more mature girlfriends had already shared this news with you, but someone had to let you know what to do hygienically when this exciting, yet frightening, situation occurred.

But the actual nitty-gritty about the sexual relationship between male and female (not necessarily between husband and wife) came to most of us from "knowledgeable" friends, dirty stories and public restroom walls.

According to the couples I see in private practice, only about two percent of them have what they consider an adequate sex education. These fortunate people had an early exposure to matters of sex, centered around Mom and Dad passing information, feelings, ideas and values to their children. One of the reasons your parents never talked to you about sex is that no one ever talked with them. Being kept in the dark was the acceptable way of life.

Let's get back to the auditorium again. People were still laughing when I asked the next question. "Now what did you call the female genitalia?" For the second time that evening a deep hush came over the audience that had been on the edge of hysteria moments before. I began to push, "OK, come on! What do we call the female genitalia?"

Finally, one woman volunteered, "We didn't call it anything in our home; we just didn't refer to it at all. It was like it wasn't there." A well-built, stocky man who looked like a Marine Corps sergeant spoke up in a loud voice, "Well, I'd tell you, Doc, but I don't think I should tell you here."

One of the reasons why this man felt that way is that most of the names we have for the female genitalia are "down there," dirty, nasty derogatory names. Now why is the male genitalia funny, but the female references are demeaning?

Superior/Inferior Attitude

Let's all imagine we are squeezed into someone's locker at high school. It's going to be a little close, but just listen. The guys are coming in from their basketball practice. One guy yells across the locker room. "Hey, Charlie! What'd you 'get' last night?" Charlie will respond that he "got" this, or a little bit of that, or he almost scored; he got to first base or second base or third base, "but I didn't hit home!"

Think of the terms guys use for sex: "conquer," "get," "score. . . ." Do these sound like loving, caring terms or do they seem absolved from the special feelings we should have toward someone in a love relationship? These young people are learning that sexual relationships are competitive; their ideas about sex indicate a *taking away from,* rather than a *giving to* another person. The question seems to be, "How much can I get?" not "How much can I give?" This is one of the results of the early teaching that sex is bad, dirty, an undiscussable subject. Naturally, forbidden fruit is all the more desirable; hence the competitive attitude.

If young people approach sex as a competitive sport, it follows that there will be an attitude of superior/inferior relationships. Somebody has to win; somebody has to lose. There is no doubt that men in our society traditionally have a superior attitude about their sexual relationship with women—that someone is *better* than someone else. To illustrate this truth, think of a dirty story for just a second. Who gets the brunt of the joke? I've asked this question hundreds of times in seminars across the country. I've learned that in a huge majority of cases it's the woman who takes the brunt of the joke; further evidence that our traditional society has really used women. *Women are not for using.* Women are for loving. *Things are for using.*

Any time sex is used as a weapon to conquer or overcome feelings of inferiority, to repay a favor, to perform a duty, to gain attention or power, or to win a battle in marriage, sex is not going to be fulfilling to the couple; as a matter of fact, it probably won't be fulfilling for either partner. In sexual relationships there are no superior/inferior roles; God *did* create the penis, it wasn't the devil's work, contrary to popular opinion in some circles. Men and women are custom-designed for each other. This is part of God's plan, and has been from the very beginning.

Men and Women are Different

Although there is no place in a marriage for superior/inferior relationships in sex, there is still the profound truth that men and women are different!

Men, we don't understand women worth squat! If I were to ask a thousand men, "What is the most special physical act a man can engage in with a woman," their response would usually be, "Ha, ha, ha, that's your question? You dummy you! Everybody knows that!"

The problem is, if I ask women that same question I am going to get a completely different answer. Men think that sex, sexual intercourse, is the most special physical act. But women will say the most special physical act is holding, just physical holding. "That's all I want. That's the most special physical act." We get into difficulty in our marriage when we begin thinking that sexual intercourse is the most important thing. These ideas we have as men are what make women tell me, "Hey, I feel used."

For the next few pages we're going to talk about how men and women are different—but equal—in their response to sexual relationships.

First of all, *men are much more readily aroused by sight than are women.* That is why magazines depicting nude women continue to flourish. However, magazines, published for women, depicting nude men will never have the staying power and interest which "men's magazines" have. Women are less likely to be sexually aroused by a good-looking man walking by, or by a nude man. My wife has always claimed that I am much sexier with my clothes on than with my clothes off. I've never tried it, but some night I'm going to sneak under the covers with my best three-piece, pinstripe suit on and bellow my mating call.

A man's time clock may start ticking at the sight of an attractive female, a suggestive picture, or a seductive look. He is easily aroused by external stimuli. Now that's not to say that some women are not aroused by the physical presence of men; that would be a ridiculous statement. But the most meaningful act a man can engage in with a woman, according to women, is just to be held, just to be physically held and prized. Anytime a husband just holds his wife without expecting anything else, she's usually in "hog heaven."

Now I know that often, after I give a lecture on this topic, there are many men who go home and say, "You know, maybe Leman has something. Marge has been a little cold the last 18 years. I'm going to try it. I'm just going to try to hold her." So he takes Marge in his arms. For a few seconds Marge is in heaven thinking, "This is wonderful, this is beautiful! He finally woke up! He sees that this is what makes me feel special."

However 4.3 seconds later his little Briggs and Stratton begins to crank up. All of a sudden—*W O M A N*! What happens to Marge at that point? She takes a nose dive. Her interest in sex and in being close to her husband has just plummeted to an all-time low.

To begin to become one in marriage, to begin to meet each other's needs we have to realize that as men and women we're different. While the old man might begin to get frisky in 4.3 seconds, it might be 43 minutes before Marge is even vaguely in the mood to be loved. There *is* a physical and psychological difference between men and women.

To correct or offset problems in marriage, the couple has to learn the skill of being close without having sexual intercourse. There need to be times when they can just cuddle up and be close, hold each other's hands, scratch each other's backs, rub each other's feet, be close, loving, caring—but no sex. Men like to be held too!

Sex Begins in the Kitchen

As I said in the first chapter, the traditional family in America today has sex in the bedroom, sandwiched between the late news and "Johnny Carson", with the lights out, the man on top of the woman.

But sex doesn't have to be in the bedroom; it can and should happen in any room in the house. Sex can be in the living room, in front of the fireplace. It can be outdoors or even in the garage (but be careful of the spiders). Sex can even be in the kitchen.

As a matter of fact, as we stated in the beginning, fulfilling, gratifying sex *begins* very often in the kitchen. For a woman to come into full expression of her feelings there has to be a certain aura around the sexual union. That aura might start in the morning when the husband remembers to take the garbage out. Or when he remembers to pick up off the floor his dirty socks and underwear. Or with any other kind of small courtesy or kindness to his family. *Sex is an all-day affair.* It starts early in the morning and culminates at a later time in a very healthy and loving way, providing the ground-work has been laid for the sexual union.

Many men have been in the business world too long. They keep talking about results. But sex isn't to be approached in a businesslike way. Neither is sex a spectator sport where one party sits back and waits for the action to begin.

For sex to be mutually fulfilling, it has to be exciting. When you've created the proper aura and conditions are just right how do you proceed to make the sex act exciting? Is it in "technique"? This is what some husbands try to tell me. But the key element in making the sex act exciting is for a man to understand that he must be gentle, loving and caring in all things. It's a matter of do you love your wife, meet her needs, put her priorities first in your life? Does she come out number one in the various facets of your life? Are you genuinely concerned about her, about her day?

Marriage is sometimes like the man who pulled into a service station and told the attendant he had a flat tire. The attendant responded, "How's your generator?"

"My generator is fine. I have a flat tire. Would you fix my flat tire, please?"

"How's your carburetor?"

"My carburetor's fine. I have a flat tire. Now would you fix the flat? I have to be at the office in 15 minutes."

My point is this: if we don't service the more *immediate* needs of our husband or wife, then we aren't going to have the opportunity to service the more intimate needs in their lives. And don't dismiss the immediate needs as unimportant.

You really have to build a track record, so to speak, to show your mate you really do care about him or her. Many husbands make the terrible mistake of telling their wives that "little things" aren't important. But, believe me, when she is home with small children all day and the washing machine doesn't work and the baby is eating a dead bug off the rug and the two-and-a-half year old gets in the oil paint, don't ever dismiss it, men, as not being important! To your wife, that's *everything*! She spent three hours trying to get green oil paint off the white bedspread. If you don't acknowledge that the "little things" in life are worthy of your attention, then you aren't going to be laying the foundation for any real communication to take place. Your wife wants to know you care about her. Getting the two-and-a-half year old to stop drinking out of the toilet is just as important as your hole in one.

So, assuming the "aura" is right for a time of satisfying

sexual relationship, now you and your mate are ready to begin loving.

Most of the men I see are really lousy lovers. Why? Because most of them assume that women are the same as men. They feel that the insertion of the penis into the vagina must be the highlight of her sex life. Not true. Actually, the most exciting part of the sex act for a woman occurs in the outer "plumbing."

I remember working with a couple, Gilbert and Ginny. They were a young couple, married approximately four-and-a-half years. I asked Gilbert if he exercised great caution and much gentleness when he stroked her clitoris.

He turned to me and said, "The whatis?" I couldn't believe what I was hearing but it became very apparent that he did not know that his wife had a clitoris. To make things worse, she didn't realize she had one either! She realized that she had some parts "down there" that were more pleasurable than others but Gilbert and Ginny had really not spent any time at all talking about their sexual needs.

Their sexual union took place in the dark, in the same room, without any conversation whatsoever, no expressions, no sweet nothings; just a sterile coming together of two robots. No wonder she described herself as feeling like a receptacle of sorts, because she certainly was.

It's important that we learn the ballpark we're playing in. It's not enough to know your own body, your own limitations, your own pleasurable zones; you also need to find what excites your mate. You have to be able to tell each other what is fulfilling for you. A woman's clitoris, in contrast to the vagina which has few nerve endings, is highly sensitive and must be touched in a very soft and gentle manner. This will bring great stimulation to your wife in a matter of minutes. But if you become too aggressive, too rough, too strong or too hurried, most women's systems will automatically shut down.

I think the neatest thing about the clitoris is that it apparently was really created for just one reason—to respond; that's the only reason for the clitoris, as far as I have been able to determine. In case I've lost you at this point, the clitoris is located where the folds of the inner lips of the vulva come together. It has tons of nerve endings, and with indirect or direct (providing it's gentle) stimulation this area fills with blood and becomes erect, much like the male penis. Usually, gently stroking the shaft of the clitoris is immeasurably stimulating for most women. It is only with gentle stimulation of the clitoral region that they are able to reach orgasm.

There has been an ugly rumor going around that there are two types of orgasms, one by way of manual stimulation of the clitoral region, the other by insertion of the penis into the vagina. I guess this rumor started because we think it would be ideal for husband and wife to reach orgasm together during the act of intercourse; however, my experience with hundreds of couples tells me that simultaneous orgasm is not very common. One person generally reaches orgasm before the other. Unfortunately, too much emphasis has been put on a couple to experience orgasm at the same time. The goal for sexual relationship should be to enjoy each other to the maximum without putting predetermined expectations on the wonderful union. It is unrealistic for a man to expect his wife to respond ultimately every time they have sex. This takes the spontaneity out of sex. If you're too busy with the rules of the game, you can't enjoy the sport! If both husband and wife reach an orgasm during intercourse it probably won't be at the same time; the wife will get there first.

Sex is not a spectator sport. Neither the wife nor the husband can sit back and wait for the mate to become orgasmic. They both have to play in the game. Men are much more easily satisfied sexually. Many of them can reach orgasm in a matter of a few seconds. Their day can be lousy, they can even be angry at their wives, upset at the boss, feeling very dejected and yet enter into a sexual relationship and reach climax in record time. But a woman doesn't have to have an orgasm every time. Many men get turned off and feel defeated if their wives don't always have an orgasm, but wives sometimes are completely satisfied with the closeness of the sexual union, the tenderness and oneness, and with meeting the needs of their husbands.

Many men grow up thinking that they have to be aggressive, rough and tumble. But when it comes to the intimate relationship of sex with one we love, what counts is a gentleness, kindness, caring and softness that really turns our mates on. Sex truly does begin early in the day, in the kitchen with a shared cup of coffee, with kind words, with thoughtfulness, with consideration, with thanksgiving, with encouraging words and actions. If all the foundations are laid properly throughout the day, women are much more inclined to sexual fulfillment.

So men, your wife really wants you to be gentle and soft and caring. But women, what do you suppose men want you to be. You guessed it! Aggressive! It's amazing to me that women are taught to be pink, unassuming, soft and submissive. Yet we find that when women become sexually aggressive it is very satisfying and stimulating to men.

Now a man likes his wife to be aggressive at certain times, but she must remember that the male genitals—especially the scrotum—are very sensitive. So gentleness is also the key to her increasing his pleasurable feelings.

I remember working with John, 26, and Karen, 24. They had been married for four years. He was now a master level student in the college of engineering, finishing up his study in electrical engineering. John was quite a student. Every night he came home and got into the same rut—ate dinner and went right to his little study desk in the hallway and began to study. Karen would try to initiate conversation only to be told to shut up. He was busy, he had to get a paper done; he had to complete a project. So, many nights Karen spent by herself watching the idiot tube while her husband studied in another part of the house.

Karen told me she felt used, that the only time John was interested in her was when *he* was frisky and ready for sex. That was the only time he expressed the I-love-you's and the I-care-about-you's to her. I asked where she felt she was on his pecking order. She said, "At best I'm second. His books and his schoolwork are certainly number one." I asked how it felt to be defeated sexually by a bunch of pieces of paper bound together in a book. She said she didn't feel very good about it. I asked her what she was prepared to do. She said, "Dr. Leman, I've tried putting on sexy nightgowns, complete with my best Estée Lauder perfume, but no results."

I said, "Well there are times I believe we really have to take the bull by the horns, take things into your own hands. What you have to do is literally take your husband's genitals in your hands." Karen looked at me with a startled expression on her face. I continued, "And I want you to make the commitment that those books are not going to win. That you are in fact going to get his attention. There's not a husband out there who doesn't want to feel that he's prized, that he's loved. But you need to become aggressive with him."

Of course her life-style was such that being aggressive did not come natural to her in any sense of the word. She had to force it upon herself. So she made the commitment, with a few suggestions from me, to greet John at the door one night with a warm kiss, to fight off the probability of his giving her a little peck on the cheek and begin looking for the mail.

Sure enough. One night he walked in the door and she firmly planted a big kiss on him. She held him so he couldn't get away and began to unbuckle his belt. The poor devil never got beyond the front hall. She took things into her own hands, literally. John later told me that was one of the greatest times they had ever had sexually—because she took action, she committed herself not to be defeated by some inanimate object.

So women, when you see your husband come home from work, let him know you are interested in his little body, right then and there. If you feel like loving, love. Or at least let him know he is very special to you and you would like to be making love to him. (Of course, if children are present you may have to let him know quietly.) Women really do have choices about how they want their mates to feel. You can make your husband feel that he is loved and prized by letting him know that you really do want him. Or you can make him feel rejected and crummy, or even indifferent, by turning him down, by emasculating him, by continually refusing his sexual advances. While we are on the subject, sometimes we can be very rude with each other in our intimate circumstances. When we're making love is not the time to point out the mistakes your lover is making. "That's all wrong" or "You really fouled that up" are not loving, inspirational words. Instead, after your time together, discuss what feels good or doesn't. But do it in a loving manner so as to bond you closer together rather than in a harsh, abrasive way that can only hurt feelings. Men need to hear from their wives that they are on the right track. It's too easy for us to try to continue a sexual relationship without any words. Rather than be a flaw-picker or completely silent in bed, try reinforcing in a positive and loving way those things that are going on that are exciting and pleasurable. Men and women both have a need to know that they are attractive, prized and special.

There's probably not a man living today who at one time or another hasn't had a fantasy or daydream about his wife meeting him at the door or chasing after him or becoming super aggressive in some way, shape, or form.

I'd like to share with you what happened to me one summer Friday evening. You know how Fridays are! You come home all hot and tired, somewhat worn out by the activities of the week. Your tie is loose and you're ready for dinner. I should have suspected from the beginning when I didn't see the children in front of the house. They usually sit out on the front rocks and vie for who will help me steer the car up the driveway. I didn't think much of it, but when I walked into the house I knew something was amiss. The dining room table was set with the best china (the one's that don't bounce back) and the stereo was on. Attached to the back of the door was a piece of red yarn which ran down to a note that was taped to the floor. The note read, "Follow this red string and you'll find a beautiful thing." So, I threw down my clothes . . . er . . . brief case and began to leisurely follow the red yarn. I followed it into the bathroom where I found another note. It said, "Not here, dummy, try the bed." Well, sure enough, there she was. My wife had gone out of her way to let me know how really special I was in her life. You would have to know my wife to appreciate the fact this is not her style.

It is safe to say that all the preparation was just for me. As we talked about it afterward, I shared with her how special she made me feel. We never did have dinner and I never found out what happened to her meal, but we had a great time by ourselves. The kids were at Grandma's house. My wife had taken the time and effort to prepare this evening for me.

What a lucky husband I am to have a wife who will go to those extremes to make me feel very special and very happy! I thank the good Lord every day for her and for what she means to me. I also tell her every day that I love her and that she means everything to me. I don't really believe "I love you" is something you can wear out in any relationship. As long as you say it in honesty, you can say it every day of the year.

(Now when I am out to a seminar I take red yarn along with me and sell it for $3.95 a foot!)

For information regarding speaking engagements or seminars, write or call:

> Dr. Kevin Leman
> 1161 N. El Dorado Place
> Suite 213
> Tucson, Arizona 85715
> (602) 886-9925

Note
1. Letha Scanzoni, *Sex Is a Parent Affair* (Ventura, CA: Regal Books, 1973), pp. 44,45.